Hope you enjoy
the adventures of the
Mystical Fairy Princess 🦋

Monique Landry Johnson

The Mystical Fairy PRINCESS

The Encounter With Dark Madness

Monique R Landry Johnson

The Mystical Fairy Princess
Copyright © 2021 by Monique R Landry Johnson

Tellwell Talent
www.tellwell.ca

ISBN
978-0-2288-5309-1 (Hardcover)
978-0-2288-5310-7 (Paperback)
978-0-2288-5308-4 (eBook)

SUMMARY

The Mystical Fairy Princess is about a young adventurous girl and her furry companion. Aaliyah spends weekends at Grandma's house. They play, they create art, and they enjoy each other's company. One day, she finds herself caught in a magical world where she meets fairies and mystical creatures and even battles a dark force that is trying to strip the colour from the world. Will Aaliyah save the people of Earth? Will Aaliyah triumph? Will the dark forces win? Come along and join Aaliyah and her new friends as they move from one end of Planet Earth to the other in a battle for their existence. I hope you enjoy the adventures of The Mystical Fairy Princess.

CONTENTS

INTRODUCTION

Dear Readers,

All my young adult life I wanted to write a book. I never really knew what kind, but being an author, well, was on my bucket list. I have always had a wild imagination, so it made it easy to delve into the mystical fantasy genre you're about to read. It took being in my fifties, and a pandemic, for me to stop and take the time to jot down ideas. My grandchildren gave me the inspiration to mingle my imagination with reality. I couldn't have done it without my family. I hope you enjoy the adventures of *The Mystical Fairy Princess* as much as I enjoyed writing them.

Monique Landry-Johnson

CHAPTER ONE

The Colourful Storm
from the Sky

T his is the story of how a beautiful young girl becomes the Mystical Fairy Princess. The little girl, let's call her by her God-given name, shall we, is Aaliyah! She is a golden-eyed beauty with a kind heart, and she has beautiful, long, curly brown hair. She spends a lot of time at her grandmother's house. She enjoys going there. She absolutely loves playing with her grandmother's dog. He has a crazy name: Graham Cracker. Told you, right... crazy! He's a goldendoodle, a very friendly and playful dog, and Aaliyah enjoys playing with him for hours at a time in her grandmother's large back yard. Best buds, you could say. Her grandmother's name is Monique. Throughout the book we will hear of the shared bond between grandmother and granddaughter. It's quite heartwarming.

One day, on November 28th to be exact, something begins to happen. The air is crisp and windy, but otherwise it is a sunny day. The trees are moving with the winds, making the branches flow like ballerinas in a row. This peaceful movement creates a symphony of beautiful melodies. Soft pleasant whispers sound throughout the woods. Aaliyah bundles up in her winter coat, hat, and mittens and proceeds to head out to the swings with Graham Cracker. The back yard of Grandmother's house borders the woods with awesome trails that lead deeper into the woods. Most weekends, Aaliyah, Grandma, and Graham Cracker hike on some of the easier trails. When Aaliyah gets older, she will conquer some of the harder ones. She loves hiking with her grandmother. When they hike, they talk about favourite foods they want to try. They discuss what pictures they want to paint on the next batch of flat rocks they find along their journey. Sometimes they just find themselves chasing Graham Cracker, because he loves to run ahead. Aaliyah loves being in the back yard with her trusty companion, Graham Cracker, as the hours pass by. On this day, they are getting ready to head in. They have played on the swings, catch, hide-n-seek, and tag. They have had a wonderful time playing outside, hardly feeling winter's chill upon them. It is getting close to the time when they have to clean up for dinner.

As they prepare to clean up the toys they have played with, and to head inside... colours begin to stream from the sky. These magnificent colours are streaming like the most colourful rainstorm one could ever imagine. Gorgeous in every way, their beauty and sound are so captivating and pleasant. There is no thought of danger; after all, they are bright, colourful, beautiful, and extraordinarily pleasant on the ears. The sounds are like an orchestra of crickets playing their invisible string instruments, or like a chorus of birds singing their sounds of lovely melodies that come so naturally from them. Those soft, gentle whispers are coming from the blowing tree limbs. They both know she is not to leave the yard without her grandmother, but with a shrug of her shoulders, Aaliyah, figuring she has Graham Cracker for protection, turns to him, saying, *"Graham Cracker, let's be real fast; Grandma won't even notice we are gone."* So they run up the path to where they can see the magnificent showing of lights. Aaliyah, knowing she is wrong to leave the yard, can't help but be pulled in that direction. Gazing at the beauty while listening to the perfectly arranged sounds, she wonders, *"What can it be?"* Aaliyah is wearing her coat with her scarf wrapped around her face. The wind, now that the day is growing older, is adding to the increasing chill. The scarf helps prevent the cooler, shrilly wind from meeting her skin. Graham Cracker is one of those dogs that grows a full winter coat and absolutely loves the cold air and snow. They both, without further thought, run towards the most spectacular viewing of lights she has ever seen. As they approach more closely, she begins to think it is an explosion of what look like butterflies, very colourful butterflies... but wait, as she stares intently, she realizes *"but it is not butterflies at all."*

"Graham Cracker," Aaliyah proclaims, *"do you see that?"*

Though Aailyah is not expecting a response, he answers, not with the normal woof but with speech. *"Yes,"* he says in human language.

"But how?" Aaliyah thinks to herself. With so much happening all at once, her focus goes back to the vision of colour blasting down from the sky. Aaliyah, completely puzzled, turns to Graham Cracker in amazement. Her large golden eyes open wide, taking in all the beauty before her. She asks, *"Did you speak? But... but how? Am I imagining this? Did you really speak?"* So many questions are swirling in her head that she feels like she is caught in a tornado of questions. Everything is happening so fast. Aaliyah's mind is spining out of control, kind of like a ride at Six Flags. You know, the kind that spins and spins and when you get off at its completion, you can't walk a straight line? Yes, exactly like that. With so many questions swirling in her mind, she mumbles, *"Is this real? Could this really be happening?"* Without thinking, she turns to Graham Cracker once again and asks, *"Are you seeing this too?"*

Graham Cracker responds *"Yes,"* once again in human English language.

Aaliyah, being the adventurous girl that she is, doesn't give much time to process that she is literally talking human with a dog. Not that talking human to a dog is crazy, people talk to their pets all the time, but this is different... really really different. He responds in human English language. Without having time to process everything all at once, she moves closer to the light show that is being presented to her. She exclaims *"Wow!"* when she sees an explosion of magnificent colour. *"What is that?"* Her eyes grow bigger, as does her smile. Aaliyah moves quickly, farther up the path, deeper into the woods. She knows she shouldn't disobey the rules of her grandmother, but she is drawn to the display of colour and continues to move even closer. She soon realizes that the lights, the beautiful colours bursting from the sky, are not butterflies. In actuality, they are odd little creatures, people, very small people with wings. In full amazement, she drops to the ground, rubbing her eyes. This is too much for her to process. *"WOW,"* she says as she hits the ground, looking up into the sky.

Graham Cracker, sitting beside her, exclaims, *"WOWSIE."*

She turns to him and says, *"How, how are you doing that? Human talk? Real words?"*

At that moment, a little winged person peeps around Graham Cracker's ear. *"Hi,"* she says, as she ducks back into Graham Cracker's hair for protection.

"Who are you?" asks Aaliyah.

"Please come out; I won't hurt you."

The little person once again pokes her head out from behind Graham Cracker and says, *"He can speak because I sprinkled magic dust on him. Only you can hear him speak human."*

As the mysterious little creature is about to hide again, Aaliyah calls out, *"Wait, who are you?"*

The creature replies, *"My name is Lillyana; they call me Lilly for short. I am a fairy. We are all fairies."*

Aaliyah calls out, *"You can come out! I won't hurt you."* Aaliyah is remaining remarkably calm, although her curiosity is peaking. *"What are fairies? Why are you here? How are you making Graham Cracker speak human? Magic dust? What's that? I'm the only one who can hear him? Why?"* Aaliyah's head fills with questions, so, so many questions...

Lilly giggles... *"It's okay, Aaliyah; I will answer all of your questions. I promise. First, I must make sure everyone has made it over safely."*

"Made it over from where?" Aaliyah is still throwing out questions. Looking up, she hears sounds of giggles coming from Lilly's direction. Now there are more little people with wings.

"Aaliyah, we are the people of Mystical Forest," says Lilly.

"Mystical Forest, hmm. I have never heard of such a place," exclaims Aaliyah.

Lilly goes on to say, *"No, you wouldn't have heard of this place. No humans know of us or of Mystical Forest."*

Aaliyah states emphatically, *"But I see you! Graham Cracker sees you!"*

"Yes," Lilly says, *"but you were chosen many many years ago, before you were even born. You come from a long line of special powers of good and beauty. You see colour, you smell beauty in the air, and you love all nature as well as animals. You have the power to keep the beauty here on Earth while..."*

"While what?" Aaliyah cries out.

Lilly, brushing off the outburst, says, *"Before I get to that, I must tell you that we have been waiting a long time to meet you. We have been watching you grow."*

"Watching me?" Aaliyah asks, puzzled and nervous. *"How? Why?"*

"Fairies can see everything," Lilly states.

Aaliyah says, *"So you were only watching me?"*

Lilly responds, *"Yes and no, but yes, kinda."* Lilly starts to get sidetracked with all of Aaliyah's questions. *"Ahem,"* Lilly clears her throat. *"We, the Fairies of Mystical Forest, knew you were the chosen one."*

"Chosen one?" repeats Aaliyah, with eyes wide open.

Lilly giggles once again and says, *"Yes, you! You are to be the Mystical Fairy Princess, our leader."*

As she swallows down hard, Aaliyah exclaims, *"I am your Princess? The Mystical Fairy Princess?"*

Lilly exclaims, *"Yes, you are our princess, and we are fairies. You were chosen as the one who can keep us safe."*

Aaliyah, caught totally off guard, calls out, *"SAFE? I am just a little girl!"*

Lilly says, *"You are more than just a little girl; you have powers. I am here to help you understand..."*

"Understand what?"

"I am here to help you understand how your powers work before the danger grows closer."

"Danger? Powers?" Aaliyah repeats with intensity.

"The Sorcerer of Darkness, Dark Madness, is trying to put our lights out. If he should succeed, people will grow lonely, depressed, nervous, and afraid. People will simply live in fear. We have known for a very long time now that you are the one who could lead us and protect us. It was prophesied that Dark Madness would someday return to Earth, spreading his darkness and sadness around the world. We knew that you would be our only chance of stopping him. We did not know when that would be, but we recently received warnings of his approach." Lilly continues, *"We need your help, Aaliyah!"* The look in Lilly's eyes unveils her true need. Her eyes seem to well up, almost in tears, as she adds, *"And we need you, Graham Cracker."* She tickles Graham Cracker near his nose. *"We need you both to stop the prophecy from being carried out."*

CHAPTER TWO

Aaliyah Meets the People...
The Very Little People...
Of Mystical Forest!

Aaliyah's first friend from Mystical Forest, as we know, is Lilly. Lilly is a cute fairy with blonde hair, porcelain skin, and blue eyes. Lilly knew that she would someday come to Earth to answer Aaliyah's questions. For years now, Lilly has been watching Aaliyah and Graham Cracker. She studied them. She watched them play. She knows what brings them the most joy. She knows what Aaliyah's favourite food is: lobster mac and cheese, of course. Let's not forget her love for chocolate. Lilly even knows Aaliyah's favourite outfit. Lilly knows everything she needs to know about the chosen one.

Aaliyah wants to bring Lilly home with her that afternoon. Aaliyah knows she has to get home before her grandmother realizes she has left the yard. Lilly tells Aaliyah that people, humankind, Earthly people... you know, like us, me and you, the reader... can't see or hear the people of Mystical Forest. She goes on to say that Aaliyah is the chosen one, that is why she can... oh yeah, let's not forget Graham Cracker can also see them. Lilly tells Aaliyah that she will meet her in her room at 10:00 p.m. that Saturday evening. Aaliyah starts winding up to throw questions out, but Lilly quickly responds, *"No, go home before your grandmother becomes suspicious. We will meet at 10:00 p.m. Saturday evening. Leave the window slightly cracked. I'll sneak in."* Aaliyah nods in assurance.

It is Friday. Aaliyah always spends the weekends at her grandmother's. On Friday nights, they eat dinner and retire early. In case you don't know what retire means, it's like saying go to bed.

On Saturday, they get up early, prepare breakfast, and travel down one of those paths that run behind Grandma's house. They look for flat rocks that have proven to be great for painting on. They search for a beautiful flower that they could look up and then press into a book to someday be made into a bookmark by melting candle or crayon pieces with the flower all between two sheets of waxed paper. By pressing this with heat, it flattens, bonds, and makes for a great bookmark. Both Aaliyah and her grandmother share a love for art. They both love colour... lots and lots of colour. Her grandmother tells Aaliyah that surrounding yourself with colour immediately puts a smile on your face. *"You can't help but feel happy,"* she says.

In the afternoon, upon return from their hike, they wash their hands and together prepare a lunch of sandwiches with a bag of chips. Their dinner is usually more elaborate. You know, like all of the food groups: meat, veggies, a side salad, and Aaliyah's favourite food group — dessert! Aaliyah does have a sweet tooth, especially for chocolate cake with chocolate pudding and chocolate candy pieces all stuck to the chocolate fudge frosting. Yum… right! Who wouldn't want a piece of that cake.

After lunch, they head into the art room to paint. The art room is Aaliyah's grandmother's favourite place to be. It helps her unwind, especially after a long day of work. They enjoy painting. They paint pictures on flat rocks like the ones I mentioned. Sometimes they paint on canvas. The art room has canvases of all sizes. It has lots of cool stuff. It's where they are allowed to express themselves to create great masterpieces. Many of the art supplies come from a local store where you can get more for your dollar. When they are planning a special piece, they go to the art store that is frequented by the local art students. Aaliyah loves going there. She loves watching the students. They are always interesting-looking, creative... Aaliyah always feels comfortable around the artsy type. More free spirits. Her grandmother recognized at a young age that Aaliyah has artistic ability. She was a very smart, early reader, and she enjoys the arts. She also is okay playing independently. She is the kind of kid who can entertain herself. Aaliyah enjoys her weekends with her grandmother and Graham Cracker. She is a bright light in her grandmother's life. They enjoy each other's company. The two share many similarities, such as their love for art and their love for the outdoors... just to name two. This past summer, they refinished some beat-up old chairs. They are awesome rocking chairs, but they were ready for the graveyard in appearance. After being refinished, they look amazing once again. Aaliyah appreciates that her grandmother allows her to be creative.

By this time, the afternoon has blown by. Grandma and Aaliyah clean up, putting away all their supplies. And once everything is in the appropriate place, they wash up and prepare dinner. Tonight's dinner is chicken breasts, Brussels sprouts, baked sweet potato, and a side salad. Grandma washes and trims all the fat (on the chicken, that is). Aaliyah seasons it. Aaliyah also washes and wraps the potatoes in aluminum foil to bake in the oven. The Brussels sprouts, well, sometimes they cook them in the oven with parmesan cheese, and sometimes they cook them in a skillet with garlic. Tonight, they are having the skillet version. Dessert will be brownies. They were baked on Friday in anticipation of Aaliyah's usual weekend ritual. By 7:00 p.m., they shower and get ready to relax in front of the television. They always share a great big bowl of popcorn with melted butter and, of course, a sprinkle of salt. They usually watch a comedy show. It warms Grandma's heart when they sit down together and share laughs. They share so many memories together. These memories continue to build with every new weekend adventure.

Aaliyah has her own room at Grandma's house. It is decorated with all of her favourite colours and things. Her bed comforter is <u>Elena of Avalor</u>, one of Aaliyah's favourite Disney Princesses. Along her bedside she has a unicorn lamp. She also has many of her best artwork pieces hanging on the walls. Aaliyah is a happy girl and loves her time at her grandmother's. She loves her room, because this space shows off her personality. Aaliyah's home life is equally great. She has a nice bedroom, great food, and wonderful parents. You know, just a wonderful life. Loving in every way that truly matters. Grandma's, well, let's just say is an adventure with all of these trails to explore, and let's not forget all the arts and crafts anyone could need. Every kid enjoys playing and painting. This life is every kid's dream. At least, this is Aaliyah's version of a wonderful life.

That Saturday night, Aaliyah tells her grandmother she wants to read a little of her book before going to sleep. This is believable because Aaliyah has been reading a book for a report due in a week. So, at 9:30 p.m., Aaliyah kisses her grandmother goodnight, proceeds to brush her teeth, and goes to her bedroom.

That night, Lilly, as promised, twinkles through the tiny space of the window opening left deliberately by Aaliyah. Twinkle is what the little winged people call it when they sneak in a small space. Really small spaces, you know, that you're like *"How did that mosquito get in?"* Aaliyah and Lilly talk all night, well until 4:00 a.m. Aaliyah, knowing that she is going to be tired in the morning, can't believe everything she is hearing. Lilly, not wanting to scare Aaliyah right from the start, decides to start with introductions. She talks about herself and the other fairies. They are all small and have wings, but they all look different as well. *"Like people on Earth,"* Aaliyah thinks to herself, *"just like us."* Lilly is very beautiful. Her blonde hair is like silk, so shiny. Her eyes are so blue, like the ocean or the sky on the most perfect day. You know, like the days that have no clouds, and you feel the sun's warmth upon your skin. That kind of perfectly blue sky. She has an adorable voice as well. An easy smooth voice. Not too high, not too low, just the right tone that makes it easy to listen. Aaliyah, even though she has so many questions, lets Lilly continue to talk.

Lilly begins by saying that they are fairies of a peaceful and loving community. They all have moms and dads, grandmas and grandpas... just like human people. But instead of living in what we believe to be a traditional home, they live in flowers or trees. Some live in water colonies. Some, yes, were born with gills as well as wings. That branch of fairies can fly and swim. Some can read minds; some have amazing strength. They have muscles, even though they are little. Aaliyah lets out a chuckle. To herself, she thinks... *"How can such a small creature be strong? After all, they are no bigger than a butterfly. How can they see the future?"* She thinks there is no way this can be, but then she quickly remembers Graham Cracker. She remembers that Lilly had made it so he could speak human language. She reflects back on the afternoon, when she watched a shower of colours rain down into the woods behind her grandmother's house. Lilly also tells Aaliyah they speak all languages. Communicating with all animals is also possible for them. Although they look like human people and talk like human people, they also have animal-like features. After all, they have wings, like a butterfly, and like I mentioned before, some have gills and swim. Lilly talks about some of the families of fairies. She describes their special powers, and she explains how each family will be instrumental in conquering the Sorcerer of Darkness, Dark Madness!!

"Okay, wait, I'm getting ahead of myself. I will get back to that, but first, gotta go back to the introductions," says Lilly. That afternoon, Graham Cracker had been calm, not his usual crazy, jumping, running, playful self. Lilly explains, *"It was fairy dust."* Aaliyah has already

witnessed that the fairy, Lilly, has powers to do so many things. Four o'clock in the morning comes fast and there is still so much that is unknown. Aaliyah knows she has to get to bed, at least for a couple of hours. Before Lilly leaves, she reassures Aaliyah that she will return.

On Sunday morning, Aaliyah sleeps in a little longer. Grandma prepares homemade waffles with all kinds of toppings, including bowls of fresh strawberries, peaches, nuts, and fresh cream. Sometimes Aaliyah's aunt and Aizen come over and join them for breakfast. Aizen is Aaliyah's cousin. Aaliyah's mom and Aunt Emily are sisters. Aizen loves waffles too. Aaliyah loves seeing her Aunt Emily. She is so much fun. During breakfast, Grandmother always says that waffles were her dad's specialty. Grandfather Bob always had the best homemade waffles as well as breakfast. Grandfather Bob's breakfasts were always a treat. Aaliyah always smiles, for she knows this herself. She has been blessed to have tasted many of Grandfather Bob's breakfasts. She enjoys Grandma's breakfasts just as much.

As much as she enjoys her weekends with her grandmother, she misses and looks forward to returning home. When Aaliyah returns home, she tells her mom all about her weekend adventures. Sarah, oh yeah, let me introduce you to Aaliyah's mom: her name is Sarah. Sarah tells Aaliyah stories of times she had with her Grandmother Doris. She thinks back to her childhood. Her grandmother always had her favourite snacks too. She loves fresh cut apples with a dash of salt. Mm...mmmm... Sarah reminisces while sharing memories with Aaliyah. This goes on for generations. Aaliyah's grandma often shares her times with her Grandmother Thérèse. Her name was funny; it had symbols in it. They would just say... *"It's French."* Okay, well, back to what we are discussing. This time is different. This time the difference is the meeting with Lilly.

CHAPTER THREE

Back Home

Aaliyah, back in her cozy room, remembers that tomorrow is Monday and she's back to school in the morning. It's currently 6:00 p.m. on a Sunday night. After Aaliyah's mom had picked her up at her grandmother's earlier that afternoon, on the way home they stopped by the farmers' market. Her mom wanted some fresh asparagus for dinner. She had marinated beef tips and prepared some white rice, and now she just needed a fresh vegetable to conclude the meal. When they get home, her mom finishes preparing dinner. Aaliyah takes a shower. After her shower, she will change into her night garments... pjs. Or pyjamas.

Usually at dinner, she tells her mom about her time at Grandma's. This time, she doesn't know what she will say. Should she mention the little people... the fairies? But *"What would Mom think?"* Aaliyah talks to herself in the shower. *"Will she think I am troubled?"*

Aaliyah's mom, listening from the kitchen, says, *"What? You okay? Are you talking to me?"*

Aaliyah quickly calls out, *"Oh no, Mom, sorry. It's just a tune I have in my head."* Aaliyah remembers that Lilly told her humans can't see or hear fairies. That night, Aaliyah, thinking aloud, says *"Who would believe me! Is everyone gonna think I'm crazy?"* So many things continue to fog up Aaliyah's head.

That night, Aaliyah chooses to keep the conversation at the dinner table about what she had painted after their hike that Saturday afternoon. Aaliyah had gone into the art room and painted a beautiful flower pattern. She loves making pictures with flowers, because it gives her an excuse to get Graham Cracker in on it. Graham Cracker will do anything for Aaliyah. He loves her as much as he loves her grandmother. On Fridays, when he hears the bus coming down the street, he knows Aaliyah is on her way. Aaliyah wonders how a dog knows it is Friday, or maybe he just hears the sound of the bus coming from the other end of the street. Country Way — that's the name of the street Grandma lives on. The bus never has a reason to travel that road except on Fridays. Grandma has prearranged that with the school for Fridays, when Aaliyah hops on bus A instead of her usual bus B. The bus driver, being an old friend of Grandma's, makes a special trip down the road and drops Aaliyah right at Grandma's door. That must be it! The bus coming down the street is like the carnival coming to town. Well, for Graham Cracker anyways. He loves playing with Aaliyah: she is young, she is exciting, and she never gets tired. They are the best of playmates. From the time Aaliyah arrives to the time she is picked up to return home, they are inseparable. Well, now that we diverted the story, let's get back to the painting that she had painted that Saturday afternoon.

Aaliyah places Graham Cracker's foot, rather his paw, in a small bowl of paint and blots it on the canvas. This makes for interesting templates for flowers. Aaliyah creates flowers out of the paw prints. Graham Cracker is always willing to help Aaliyah in any way he can. He absolutely loves her and she loves him just as much. Thank goodness for the cement floor in the art room. Paint has already marked the floors, giving the room an even more artsy feel. You know... like all the pieces created there are done by artists transposing ordinary canvas into magnificent works of art.

Sarah, Aaliyah's mom, has started the conversation at the table. Aaliyah's dad has to work a travelling job, and he won't be home until Monday evening. Armani, Aaliyah's brother, has taken the ride with his dad. So, it's just Mom and Aaliyah tonight.

Mom starts, *"So, Aaliyah, what did you do at Grandma's this weekend?"*

Aaliyah, once she has finished her bite of beef tip and rice, responds, *"Well we took a walk/ hike, collecting flat rocks on the way."* In her upbeat tone, she goes on to say, *"We did find one plant that had flowered beautifully. Grandma didn't recognize it. We snapped a photo of it and Grandma was gonna look it up, research it. It would make an awesome-looking bookmark."* Aaliyah exclaims joyfully, *"You know Grandma; she wanted to make sure it wasn't poisonous or something before we touched it."*

Aaliyah goes on to tell her mom what they made for dinner. Then, she talks about the painting she made with Graham Cracker. She chuckles as she remembers the paw print paint mess that they added to the other floor markings. She says, *"Maybe I'll make flowers on the floor someday out of all the paw prints and various other paint splatters."* Both Mom and she laugh. Before they know it, dinner is done.

Sometimes Armani goes to Grandma's too. He only goes once a month. Armani is 12 and he loves to play his PlayStation game system. His friends and cousins on his dad's side, the boys, that is, all play online. Today, kids don't need to go to a friend's house to play. They interact and play against each other online, through the internet. Who would have thought people would be able to communicate and actually play games against each other while residing in different places. If you ask me, yes, it's pretty cool, but it makes it easy to be lazy. Give me a good old-fashioned bike or a walking stick for a hike.

Aaliyah helps her mom bring the dishes to the sink and load the dishwasher. Another one of those gadgets that make life easier. I'm not going to lie; I would miss my dishwasher if I ever had to live without it. Aaliyah, being extra tired, after all, she had a most interesting weekend, only getting to bed at 4:00 a.m. the evening before, tells her mom that she wants to go to bed without watching TV. Mom asks, *"Are you feeling well?"*

"Yes, I'm just tired from all the fresh air and chasing my big furry friend," says Aaliyah while giggling. Little girls giggle about everything. So, she kisses her mom goodnight and off to her room she goes. Within minutes, Aaliyah is fast asleep. Her mom checks in on her. *"Yup, out like a light,"* says Mom in a whisper. *"I guess she did get a lot of fresh air, and now she's already sleeping. Sweet dreams, my beautiful princess."* Mom goes into the living room, watches a TV show, and retires early herself. *"My, I think I'm equally as tired as Aaliyah. And I had no fresh air or dog-chasing activities."* As she tucks herself under her blanket, she stretches out with a sigh. *"Ahhhh, this is nice."* Seeing that Aaliyah's dad won't be home for another day yet, she takes advantage of the extra space.

The next morning, Mom, like on every weekday morning, opens Aaliyah's bedroom door. *"Rise and shine, sunshine!"* she says in her most cheerful voice. Aaliyah is a morning person. She enjoys when the sun rises and shines through her bedroom window first thing in the morning. Once Aaliyah hears Mom's wake-up call, she pops out of bed and immediately goes to the kitchen table for breakfast. Mom has it ready. She loves that cereal with the leprechaun marshmallows. Hmmm... think it's called Lucky Charms. Yes, that's it: Lucky Charms. Personally, I think the marshmallows are hard, but Aaliyah enjoys them. Sometimes she has French toast sticks, the kind with sprinkled cinnamon, and Mom heats up a small dipping dish of maple syrup.

After breakfast, Aaliyah goes back to her room to get dressed. Then, she goes off to the bathroom to comb her hair and brush her teeth. By 7:30 a.m., Aaliyah, with backpack in hand, is seated in the car, seat-belted. They live 15 minutes from the school. Mom drives them in but they take the bus home. Armani will be absent today because he is on the road trip with Dad. Dad was making a delivery to one of the other sister stores in the chain he works for. From time to time, Armani and Aaliyah make the trip with him. Dad takes advantage of the time he has with them by talking, seeing where their heads are at. They talk about school and friends.

Mom drops her off at school. Aaliyah begins to think of the fairy encounter. *"Was this real?"* she thinks aloud. Lilly said she would return. Aaliyah still has her doubts. *"Was it all a dream?"* You know... the kind when you have no idea you are sleeping. You wake up and you truly think you just lived through that, like a scene in a movie you watched. Vivid, so vivid. Furthermore, you wake up tired because your mind has tricked your body into feeling like you ran that race, or had a dance recital and you were the star. Or, in the case of Aaliyah, witnessed a fairy encounter of the magnificent kind. She is very distracted in school today. She can't help wondering when or if Lilly is going to return. The bigger question is... had she dreamt the whole thing? Was it all a dream?

Aaliyah goes about her day, and the next, then the next, hardly giving any more thought to the fairies and the impending danger that Lilly had spoken of. On Thursday morning, she starts thinking again. She hasn't seen any signs of Lilly. To herself, she thinks, *"Hmmmm... maybe I did just have a vivid dream. I must have just imagined the whole thing."* Quickly, she resolves herself to thinking, somehow, *"Yes, this was all just a dream."* Aaliyah, being eight years old, quickly does just that... puts it behind her and acts like every eight-year-old girl. Normal, no powers, no super-strength, no mind-reading.

Friday comes along and Aaliyah, like every Friday, takes the appropriate bus that brings her right to Grandma's front door. Aaliyah skips down the walkway to the front door, which Grandma has left open to watch for her arrival. Graham Cracker sits right in the doorway. Aaliyah chuckles to herself... *"Hehehe... wonder what wild dreams I am gonna live out this weekend. Must be all the extra sweets I get; Grandma does indulge me."* She shrugs her shoulders in an *"oh well"* gesture and walks in. *"Hi, Grandma."*

Grandma, hearing Aaliyah as she enters the front door, replies, *"I'm here, in the kitchen."* Graham Cracker immediately greets Aaliyah with big wet kisses.

CHAPTER FOUR

Will Lilly Return or was it All Just a Dream?

Aaliyah is greeted by many kisses from Graham Cracker. Grandma runs to the phone as Aaliyah is walking into the house. She waves quickly from the kitchen. It is a portable phone, but it had been placed on the cradle. That's what they call the base it sits on to charge. Graham Cracker looks at Aaliyah and says, *"I missed you."*

Aaliyah, immediately caught off guard, exclaims, *"It wasn't a dream! OMG! Let me put my books in my room. Let's go to the swings; we can talk there!"* As she heads to her room, she thinks, *"Here I go again, talking human to a dog."* She rolls her eyes and smiles. *"Worse, actually, the dog is talking to me in human. Just when I had explained the whole experience away as a very elaborate dream."* She throws her books down on her bed.

Aaliyah, seeing Grandma is still on the phone, signals to her that she and Graham Cracker are going outside. It gets dark early. Winters in New England are cold and short. There isn't much time to play outside on Fridays by the time Aaliyah gets home from school. It gets dark as early as 4:30 p.m. in the winter; that doesn't leave much time. The temperatures are really beginning to grow colder as they approach the winter months. They don't mind; they love playing outside. Today, most kids don't play outside as much as kids of the past. Armani prefers being in his room playing his portable game system. Grandma tells him she is saving up to buy him a big console that they will keep hooked up at Grandma's house. This way he will be all set up and have no reason not to want to come. Grandma realizes that kids are different today. Their interests are vastly different than when she was a child. Being okay with that, she is okay with making their rooms comfortable. She just enjoys her time with them, even if Armani only comes out to eat dinner.

Grandma acknowledges that she is aware of Aaliyah and Graham Cracker heading out to play. Aaliyah puts on her warm winter coat. She has two winter coats. She generally wears the warmer one to Grandma's because that's where she spends more time outside. During the week, she wears the more streamlined, less puffy coat. It is better for the car and in-and-out errands. So, she is now bundled in the warm coat, hat, mittens, and scarf. She wraps the scarf around her face to stop the punch of New England weather. Some New England days are bitter cold with negative temperatures and the wind blowing. The "wind chill," the guy on the TV called it. Aaliyah hears this when her mom and Grandma watch the local news. Aaliyah sometimes pretends to be a television celebrity or weather person, copying some of their words and using a whole lot of hers. She is a happy girl.

Aaliyah starts swinging on the swing set. She loves to swing, no matter the season. Graham Cracker runs around and around. He is just happy to have company with him. Graham Cracker loves the cold air and snow even more. It hasn't snowed yet this year.

Aaliyah yells, *"Graham Cracker, come here."*

He quickly runs to her and says, *"Yes? What would you like?"*

Aaliyah, while talking to the dog, knows that it wasn't a dream. She sits in silence for a few seconds. She begins, *"Did we really see that explosion of colour? Did we see the fairies of Mystical Forest rain down before us?"*

Graham Cracker, his head tipped at an angle, says, *"Yes, and Lilly was real nice. She tickled my ear."*

"So I didn't imagine it," she says as she rubs her head, *"but Lilly never contacted me, nothing, all week. She said she would return, that she would be in touch. It's been a week!"* Both Aaliyah and Graham Cracker instinctively look up the path. Everything looks normal. Same old dirt paths, no fantastic colours. Just woods, lots of woods.

An hour has gone by now. It's just about 4:30 p.m. and growing darker. One moment it's bright and sunny, and the next moment it's dark. Aaliyah calls to Graham Cracker, who has decided to take another run around the yard. *"Let's go inside and see what's for dinner."* While they were out playing, looking for any signs of Lilly or any of the fairies for that matter, Grandma has been preparing one of Aaliyah's favourite meals.

Aaliyah says, *"What's for dinner, Grandma?"*

Grandma answers, *"What's it smell like, princess?"*

Oh yeah, I forgot to mention that Grandma often refers to Aaliyah as a princess, a pet name. Who could have known she really is a live princess? The Mystical Fairy Princess!

Aaliyah says, *"Mmmm... I think it's my favourite, macaroni and cheese."*

Grandma says, *"Yes, and I defrosted some lobster..."* (that she had cooked and preserved during the summer, but before Grandma could finish...)

Aaliyah says, *"Oh... lobster macaroni and cheese, my favourite. Thanks, Grandma."*

Grandma, knowing what Aaliyah's reaction will be, continues, *"And for dessert, chocolate cake, with chocolate pudding inside, double fudge frosting, and I saved the chocolate pieces for you to stick to the frosting on the sides of the cake."*

Aaliyah says, *"Oh, thank you, Grandma. All my favourites tonight."*

Grandma is older now with fewer commitments. Well, maybe not, but she always makes time for her grandchildren. She loves each and every one of them equally. She enjoys and loves the time she spends with them and they love her just as much.

After dinner, Aaliyah takes her shower then retires to the living room to watch a TV program. Then, she decides to read a new book she had picked up at the library. It is about unicorns. It drew her attention because the cover had a unicorn with wings, like Lilly. She wonders if unicorns come from Mystical Forest. *"But how?"* she thinks. Humans can't see mystical people. She tilts her head and scrunches her eyebrows. *"But I did, and here is a book about a unicorn. I even have a unicorn lamp and a unicorn stuffed toy. Hmmm."* She kisses Grandma and goes to her room, Graham Cracker trailing behind her. Grandma smiles and continues to watch her Friday night shows followed by the 10 o'clock news.

Aaliyah gets to her room and decides, even though it is very cold, to leave her bedroom window cracked open slightly, just enough in case Lilly returns. Aaliyah wonders if that could be why Lilly didn't or maybe couldn't return. She hadn't remembered to keep her window cracked open. Graham Cracker jumps on the end of her bed and asks, *"Will you read to me, Aaliyah?"* He rests his head at the foot of the bed and looks up at her. Aaliyah nods and then proceeds to prop her pillows up. She begins.

"Barbie and The Magic Pegasus is the name of the book." She proceeds to read with Graham Cracker listening intently. *"Barbie takes flight in her first original princess fairytale, Barbie and The Magic Pegasus. Princess Annika (Barbie) discovers adventures when she is befriended by Brietta... a magnificent winged horse... that flies her to the beautiful cloud kingdom... wizard... forbidden forest... Beethoven's Sixth Symphony... fly... amazing adventure,"* Aaliyah says as she shifts her eyes from the book to Graham Cracker. *"Doesn't that sound like what happened to us? Well, kinda, anyways. There are many similarities."*

She continues to read to Graham Cracker until her eyelids weigh heavy. She marks her page with one of her beautiful pressed flower bookmarks. Then, she places the book on her nightstand. As she turns the knob on the lamp off, she says, *"Goodnight, Graham Cracker. I love you."*

He looks at her and replies in his young man voice, *"I love you more."* Graham Cracker has a happy voice with a fun-to-be-around temperament. It's true that dogs are emotional beings, possessing a hormone called oxytocin. This hormone allows feelings of love and affection for others. So, Graham Cracker doesn't say this out of recognition from hearing it. He says it from the heart. They really do love each other. This is one of the things Lilly noticed about them: their mutual love for each other. True caring. Aaliyah, once again, must be reflecting on Lilly's words, for she is scrunching her eyebrows, like she often does when thinking. The two drift off into a sleepy slumber.

The next morning, they rise early, as they do every Saturday morning. Grandma likes to hit the trail early, leaving plenty of afternoon time for other projects. In the morning, you are more likely to catch viewings of bunnies hopping or a deer grazing. The turkey sightings are always interesting. They stroll like they own the area, with no cares. Turkeys strut with their heads up, allowing their feathers to make a statement. They can be noisy too at times. Grandma and Aaliyah go down to the kitchen for egg sandwiches. Grandma drinks her coffee and Aaliyah drinks hot chocolate. Once they are done, they bundle up for their journey down one of the paths. They always carry their backpacks in case they came across some cool findings. They are venturing up the same path as last week. Grandma has done her research on that mysterious flower that they saw. It appears to be a Hellebores flower. Hellebores plants are also known as Lenten roses. Grandma tells Aaliyah, *"Despite their delicate appearance, they're tough as nails."* That means super-duper hard. Grandma is surprised to have never come across this flower before.

They collect beautiful flowers and pretty leaves to press in a book and later make into bookmarks. They find two awesome flat rocks as well. If you paint on rocks, you will understand. The flatter the rock, the easier to paint a scene, but sometimes a jagged rock can produce some interesting pieces. It all depends on how creative you want to get. Grandma and Aaliyah belong to a rock group. They paint their rocks and post a picture to a site. When you find a rock that has been painted by another member, you also post a picture of the wonderful rock art to show the members it has been found. You can keep it or re-hide it for someone else to find. This kind of keeps the fun going. All the rocks usually get tagged to the rock group, so newcomers can sign in and play along as well. Today, they also collect some princess pine. They discuss making homemade wreaths for Grandma's as well as Mom's front door. Grandma always has great fun planned. It's never boring at Grandma's house.

They clean up and make a couple of burgers along with French fries in the air fryer. Oh, and let's not forget: a slice of chocolate cake from last night... *"Yummmm,"* says Aaliyah. Once lunch is done, they set up the table to make their wreaths. The afternoon seems to fly by. Time to shower already. No prep time for dinner tonight. Grandma had seen a pork chop slow cooker recipe. She had been wanting to try it and decided today was as good a day as any. Time to retire to the living room and watch their Saturday night lineup. Once they have digested their dinners, they share a buttery batch of popcorn. At 10:00 p.m., Aaliyah kisses Grandma goodnight and retires to her room. As always, Graham Cracker follows right behind her.

Once again, while brushing her teeth, Aaliyah thinks, *"Hmmmm, I gotta remember to open the window slightly, just in case Lilly returns."* Aaliyah immediately lays her head on her pillow and says, *"Sorry, Graham Cracker, no book tonight."* She nods off quickly. Suddenly, she feels a tickle. She keeps swiping at her nose — again, a tickle. *"Graham Cracker, stop, I'm trying to sleep."* Realizing Graham Cracker is lying at her feet, she pops upright, eyes wide open. She sees that Lilly has returned but she isn't alone this time.

Lilly, in her perfectly toned voice, says, *"Aaliyah, it's me, Lilly."*
Aaliyah is still trying to focus.

Lilly says, *"Hi, Aaliyah!"*

Aaliyah asks, *"What happened?"*

"What do you mean?"

"It's been a week; I haven't heard from you."

A young person seems to suspend in time. You know, to an adult, Christmas each year comes faster and faster. To a child, it seems to take forever.

Lilly says, *"Yes, I know, but we have been very busy. We have been gathering information that has surfaced. That is why I brought Aizen with me."*

Aaliyah says, *"Aizen? That's different. No one but my cousin has that name. His name is Aizen too. I never heard of anyone else having such a name. Maybe it's not an uncommon name after all."*

Lily says, *"Yes. He is our communicator. He has been receiving intel that the Sorcerer of Darkness, Dark Madness, can morph into a human form here on Earth. The intel Aizen received specifically states that he goes by the name Daryl... this we knew already."*

Aaliyah, with a look of confusion, repeats, *"Daryl? Huh?"*

Aizen says, *"Yes, I received reports that he has been spotted here on Earth. We obtained a confidential video where he transforms from his evil Dark Madness self into a regular-looking guy named Daryl."* Aizen is a very smart and powerful person. He looks small and stocky. He has a grumpy disposition. All work and no play kinda guy.

Aaliyah is even more confused. *"Daryl? I have an uncle named Daryl. My cousin Aizen's dad."*

Lilly says, *"So sorry, Aaliyah, but I told you I would be back and I am here now! We have a lot of work to do."*

CHAPTER FIVE

The Mission Begins to Develop

L illy and Aizen are in Aaliyah's bedroom. Aaliyah gets out of bed, when they arrive, grabs her bathrobe and moves to her desk quietly. She doesn't want to disturb her grandmother. If Grandma hears them, she will say she is reading her book aloud and that she got to a really good part and couldn't put it down. Grandma, being an avid reader, would understand getting to a part that you just couldn't put it down. Graham Cracker is sitting beside her. Lilly and Aizen are flying around, sometimes pausing in midair. At times it appears as though they are resting but their wings are still moving. Sometimes their wings stop, but they remain suspended in air.

"Really weird," Aaliyah exclaims aloud.

"What's weird?" asks Aizen instantly. In defence, he zooms towards Aaliyah, practically touching her nose. She pulls back without hesitation.

Lilly hurries to say, *"NO NO, it's okay. He won't hurt you, Aaliyah. He just, well, is very protective of our people. He is young. He is not only a communicator; he is a mind reader. He can perform mental telepathy. It is a rare trait, but it is most important. He can see the future."*

"That's so cool," Aaliyah exclaims, more bright-eyed than ever. She couldn't help but react. She knows there is danger looming, but her interest is piqued. She wants to know more, despite the danger. She should have wanted to shut her window, lock it, and possibly board it up. Stay completely away from any of this fairy, forest, and Dark Madness talk.

"What's weird?" exclaims Aizen again.

Aaliyah chuckles. *"It's not bad. I was just amazed at how your wings move if you are moving and sometimes stop if you're not. How you can suspend in air with no breeze. Told you, not bad."* Aaliyah gives him a forward head gesture, almost touching his nose.

Lilly comments, *"Boy, these two are a match, ready to lock horns."* That means ready to argue. *"I truly hope you grow to like each other, or at least tolerate each other, because we have lots of work to do!"*

The four make plans to meet at the treehouse in the back yard. The treehouse is really cool. It goes up a big oak. Grandma nailed wood across for stairs. When you reach the floor, you just pull yourself up. Sounds harder than it is. There are handles at the top, nailed into the floor for leverage. It has closed walls. Inside, Aaliyah keeps a blanket, a pillow, a couple of books, and one of her stuffed toys. One of her favourites, actually. *"Hmmmm..."* the narrator thinks... *"Wonder why she leaves it all in the treehouse?"* Anyways, Grandma makes sure her items are kept bug-free and smelling clean. She stores them in a closed bin, and she places a fresh dryer sheet inside as well. Every once in a while, Grandma grabs these items, washes them, dries them, and replaces them back up into the treehouse.

"So, we will meet at 10:00 a.m. at the treehouse," calls out Lilly while twinkling through the crack in the window. Aizen has already twinkled through.

"Tomorrow, yes tomorrow!" Aaliyah calls out, forgetting about what time it is and that Grandma is in the next room sleeping. She doesn't hear. Aaliyah sighs, pushing her hair from her face. *"Come, Graham Cracker, to bed!"*

"Graham Cracker loves you, Aaliyah," he says in a kindly tone. *"Goodnight! Zzzzzzzz."*

The next morning, when they wake up, Aaliyah says, *"I'm so hungry. Let's go eat, Graham Cracker."* Off to the kitchen they go. Grandma has gotten up early, and she surprises Aaliyah with a garden vegetable omelette. Sometimes Aaliyah likes her omelette with hot sauce, and sometimes she likes her omelette with real maple syrup — not the kind with artificial flavouring, either. The kind of maple syrup you get from tapping a tree: pure and so rich-tasting. When Grandma adds bacon and sausage to Aaliyah's omelette, she likes the maple syrup best. Today is hot sauce. Grandma has a couple of potatoes, so she makes up some hash browns too.

Aaliyah says, *"Oh thank you, Grandma."*

Grandma says, *"You're welcome, princess."*

Aaliyah says, *"I woke up so hungry. I must have run a race in last night's dream."*

Grandma says, *"I see it made for a ravenous appetite."*

Aaliyah says, *"It smells so good!"*

Aaliyah, licking her lips, washes her hands and sits at her place at the table. They eat, and once they are done, Aaliyah helps Grandma clear the table.

Grandma says, *"It's okay, Aaliyah; I got this. You can go play with Graham Cracker. Hope you didn't mind that we didn't have waffles this morning. It's just that I had so many vegetables from the farmers' market and I didn't want to waste them. I know you love your waffles and fixings."* Grandma smiles.

"No," Aaliyah calls out, *"it was delicious."*

Aaliyah dresses warmly in her coat, hat, mittens, and scarf wrapped across her face. In a muffled voice, talking through her scarf, she yells out, *"Playing in the treehouse, Grandma"* as she goes out the door with Graham Cracker.

I bet you're wondering how Graham Cracker will get up to the treehouse. Well, over time, as Aaliyah and Graham Cracker became practically inseparable, he wanted to go up. He would cry down below the whole time Aaliyah played up there. Now, a ramp coming from the backside comes down for him. It can only be dropped from the top. Once Aaliyah gets up there, she lowers the steps by a pulley. It was made this way so that unwanted creatures from the woods won't just stroll on up. When they aren't being used, the stairs remain up. Now that Aaliyah and Graham Cracker are up in the treehouse, she sits at the table. Graham Cracker sits beside her.

Aaliyah says, *"It's 9:55 a.m.; they should be here soon."*

In a puff... poof... Aizen splashes out. There is no water, of course, but it is like splashing through the air. Puff... poof... Lilly appears. *"Right on time,"* Lilly exclaims. *"We must get right to work. It is imperative we strategize before Dark Madness gets the jump on us."*

Aaliyah asks, *"What do we need to do?"*

Aizen answers, *"We need to bring you to Mystical Forest where you can learn more quickly than you can here. In fact, it's impossible to train you here. Our technology and abilities are superior to yours. We are light-years ahead of humans."* Aizen shoots a slighted look over his shoulder, as he looks back at her. You know, that smarty-pants kinda look... like, "Ha, what do you think of that?" with his head moving from side to side. A "know-it-all" look!

Aaliyah, rolling her eyes, says, *"Here we go again, ugh."* Aaliyah wonders how she can go to Mystical Forest when she can't leave the back yard.

Aizen says, *"We take you through the portal."*

Aaliyah asks, *"But, but, how did you?"*

Aizen explains, *"I read minds, remember?"* Yes, this is a question, but it is more like a statement. Aizen is a very direct, angry-sounding, irritable, cranky kinda fellow.

Aaliyah, under her breath, mumbles... *"Know-it-all!"*

Graham Cracker chuckles in a woofy way. Like, *"Urff urff."* That is a funny laugh. I guess it really isn't, considering it's a talking human language laughing dog. Aizen is not amused. He just sends a disapproving look to the two of them.

Aaliyah says, *"What if Grandma comes out to check on us? She often does."*

Lilly says, *"We can portal you back through in seconds! We can see everything from the Forest that's happening here, on Country Way. You will see; we will show you."*

Aaliyah says, *"Oh, okay. Let's Gooo!"* She raises her arms in the air. *"We can do this!"* she yells out, like a New England cheerleader cheering on the spectators of a Patriots football game.

Through the portal the five go. *"Wait a minute; there were four that transported. What's going on?"* Aizen stares over at Aaliyah.

Lilly is confused. She says, *"It doesn't make sense. There are four of us."*

Aizen, now realizing the problem, really glares at Aaliyah. *"Hmmm, yup, it's her again!"*

Lilly says, *"Aizen, stop, why would you say that?"*

Aizen says, *"Look in her hand."*

Aaliyah says, *"What? My stuffed toy? I didn't know I had her in my hand at the treehouse. She's my favourite."*

Remember me telling you about Aaliyah's favourite toy in the treehouse? Aaliyah, without giving it any thought, always grabs her toy whenever she is up there. Her unicorn stuffed toy has a colourful horn and pastel wings. She has a pink heart marking on her rear hip. She is a female unicorn with pink hair. So, when they transported over, Abigail the unicorn, but Aaliyah calls her Abby for short, transported with them. But when she transported, she was no longer a stuffed toy; she was already beginning to change. She has now come to life as a mystic creature. Aaliyah nervously drops her as she grows in size.

Aaliyah says, *"She is alive, as big as Graham Cracker. So beautiful, really really beautiful."* Aaliyah is mesmerized by what she was seeing.

Abby begins to move and talk. She says, *"Hi, Aaliyah, I finally can tell you all the things I couldn't. You would talk to me, hug me, and now I can answer back with the care and love you have always shown me."*

Aaliyah's mouth opens. *"WOW"* comes out as she stands there with her golden eyes so wide. *"She's so beautiful."*

Graham Cracker says, *"WOWSIE."*

Lilly says, *"Well, this solves one problem. We will send her to school and she can learn all about transporting. We can give her a few other talents that will be useful in conquering the sorcerer. Lucky girl."* Lilly pats her gently on her nose. *"You are very fortunate to become one of us!"* Abby smiles joyfully.

Aizen says, *"And the big furry guy, he's going to obedience school?"*

Lilly says, *"Aizen,"* as she shoots him a stern look.

Aizen says, *"Okay, I meant transport school as well."*

Lilly says, *"Yes, both will go to transport school. Abby, we will be teaching you a few extra things as well."* Lilly continues, *"Aaliyah, you will be coming with Aizen and myself."* Lilly yells, *"Come on, we need to drop Graham Cracker and Abigail at the Morgan-Rizzo Transport School. It's the best training school in the land."*

They make their way to the Morgan-Rizzo Transport School and home where the instructors Michelle, Samantha, Amanda, Vanessa, and John will train Graham Cracker and Abigail to transport. The school usually teaches the new fairies and any other newcomers to twinkle — remember, how they get through small cracks — and puff... poof... through portals. They also are taught, or should I say trained, in the ability to grow massive in size and then return to natural size. Being able to grow or shrink comes in handy, depending on the circumstances. You never know when you may need to hide. The success rate of that school is very good. The best trained soldiers go there.

Lilly says urgently, *"We are pressed for time. We must hurry. Approximately 20 minutes ago, intel came in that Dark Madness was heading towards Planet Earth. Tristan just communicated the information through the telecommunication device."*

Aaliyah gasps, *"What do we need to do?"*

In his raspy, rough tone, Aizen chimes in, *"We need to get to work! No time for idle chit-chat. That's what we need to do."*

Lilly says, *"Aizen... uggh, be nice. We are kind creatures."* Aizen, feeling a little sensitive, moves a bit ahead, still heading in the direction of the school. He doesn't like others to see when he is in distress.

Michelle is outside of the Morgan-Rizzo facility.

Michelle says, *"Hi everyone."*

Lilly says, *"We have two students: Graham Cracker and Abigail. You should have received the paperwork. I sent it over when we checked in. I sent it ahead so you would be aware and we could immediately move on to the Hubble."*

Amanda, one of the school trainers, says, *"Yes, I have it."* She flies out, waving the papers in her hand. *"Here it is."*

Aizen says, *"Let's go, people."*

Aaliyah says, *"He really is a grumpy one, even though he is from such a happy, positive, colourful place."*

Lilly says, *"When we have more time and are not facing an attack from a very powerful sorcerer, I will tell you that story."*

Lilly, Aizen, and Aaliyah make their way to the Hubble. The Hubble is their control centre. All information that comes to each fairy home is first communicated through the main Hubble. This way, the overseers compile all the data. Aizen, because of his ability to see the past, can see all of the events that lead up to current situations. With his ability to see the future, he can put a plan into action that will potentially alter the course of what could happen. They are hoping Aizen will be able to outsmart the encounter with Dark Madness.

"What is Daryl the Dark Sorcerer trying to do, exactly?" asks Aaliyah.

Lilly says, *"Our colours,"* as a teardrop streams from her eye down her cheek.

Aaliyah says, *"I don't understand."*

Lilly says, *"Without colour, everything is dark and gloomy. So if he succeeds, not only will everyone turn sad and disgruntled, but the world, stripped of colour, will begin to die off too. Trees will start to rot; animals won't be able to feed. The world as you know it will not be the same. We will all become extinct. We will be gone, along with Mystical Forest."* Aizen turns away, weeping.

Aaliyah thinks to herself, *"Wow, that's the first sign of emotion I have seen from him."* She refrains from gazing at him or commenting. She can see he is just a little boy. *"Boy, does he have a lot of responsibility, though,"* she thinks silently. She is obviously forgetting that one of the other things Aizen can do well is read minds. Aaliyah can't remember everything that is happening. Mind you, it is all happening so quickly.

All of a sudden, Aaliyah begins brainstorming. The three of them huddle for hours, occasionally calling upon other members of the community with their own sets of powerful skills. They are brought in to give their professional opinions at different points during the meeting.

Aaliyah, being so wrapped up in what she is doing and learning, stops as panic hits her. *"My grandma. How long has it been? Is she looking for me? Grandma will worry; I can't do that to her."*

Lilly explains, *"No! time works differently here. It moves here much faster than it does on Earth. Warp speed. It's only been like five minutes Earth time."*

Aaliyah says, *"Phew... okay, let's get back to this."* As she moves to get comfortable and back to the plans, she asks, *"You can see Grandma's house and what's happening back home, in North Smithfield, Rhode Island? Someone is keeping track?"*

Aizen replies, *"Yes, already"* in his usual grumpy way.

Time continues to pass as they devise what they hope to be a foolproof strategy. They are hopeful that it will protect them from the evil sorcerer's wrath. Now it is time to get Aaliyah and Graham Cracker home before Grandma notices their disappearance.

Lilly says, *"I'm gonna bring you and Graham Cracker back. Aizen has lots of communications to retrieve. Abby will remain as well. She will be staying here at the Morgan-Rizzo Transport School. Samantha and Vanessa will be continuing to teach her the extra powers we spoke of.*"

Lilly, Aaliyah, and Graham Cracker run over to the transport station. Graham Cracker, knowing what he needs to do, taps the button that magnetically opens the portal. Lilly notices Aaliyah watching. She says, *"That's one of the things he was taught."* She smiles. *"You will notice many things that he can now do, like flying..."*

They all jump through the portal... Puff... poof... Graham Cracker comes through first... puff... poof... Aaliyah falls to the ground. Lastly, puff... poof... Lilly. All three are back in the treehouse.

Aaliyah says, *"How are we gonna get together? I go back home tonight. Graham Cracker lives here. It's only on weekends we are together."*

Lilly says, *"Graham Cracker knows exactly what to do. Sometimes it might be Abigail who transports you. Tomorrow at 10:00 p.m., Graham Cracker will twinkle through your window and bring you to the Hubble."* She snickers and chuckles. *"It's both difficult and hilarious picturing Graham Cracker, the 103-pound dog, sneaking through a crack,"* she apologizes as she chuckles still.

"That will be a sight," says Aaliyah.

Lilly continues, *"It will feel like six hours, but will only be one hour on Earth time. So don't worry, Aaliyah, you will be home in time to sleep. You will be bright-eyed and bushy-tailed for school in the morning."* That's an old saying that means you will be rested and alert, ready for anything, like a squirrel.

Aaliyah says, *"Okay, thank you, Lilly... bye!"* She waves as Lilly transports back. *"Come on, Graham Cracker, go down the ramp so I can pull it up."*

"Okay," he says as he runs down. Aaliyah pulls up the ramp and then looks around, putting everything in its place. Almost everything, anyways. She remembers that her favourite toy, her beautiful unicorn, is now a mystical creature — one of the most beautiful she has ever seen. Abigail is now a beautiful, most-powerful, mystical player in the strategy. *"Who would have thought?"*

Aaliyah says. She stands, ready to go down the wooden nailed-in boards that function as steps, but then she turns her head to check one last time. *"Yup, all is good."* Down she goes. *"Come, Graham Cracker, Mom will be here soon to pick me up."*

Grandma asks, *"Did you have fun, princess?"*

Aaliyah says, *"Yes, we were playing make-believe. We pretended to be fighting an evil villain."*

Grandma says, *"Sounds fun. Wasn't too cold for you out there?"*

Aaliyah says, *"No, I didn't even notice the cold."* Thinking to herself, she reflects, *"I can't remember thinking anything about the weather."* Puzzled, her brow wrinkles. She shakes it off and shrugs her shoulders. *"I just can't remember."*

Grandma asks, *"Would you like a snack?"*

Aaliyah says, *"Yes... cut apple?"*

Grandma says, *"Of course, coming right up, with a dash of salt."*

Aaliyah says, *"Thanks, Grandma."*

Grandma says, *"You're welcome. Here you go, Aaliyah. Don't worry, Graham Cracker, I didn't forget about you."* Grandma bends over to place a paper plate with a cut apple on the floor for Graham Cracker.

They eat their apples while watching a TV show. When Mom arrives to pick her up, Aaliyah runs over to Grandma and says, *"Thank you for making my favourites."*

"Here's Mom," Grandma says.

Aaliyah says excitedly, *"Hi, Mom. Look at what we made. I made it for your outside door out of the princess pine we collected."*

Sarah says, *"Wow, princess, that's so nice and it smells so good. I almost hate to leave the great pine smell for the outside."* She grins warmly at her daughter. Aaliyah, feeling accomplished, is happy about the fuss her mom is making.

Aaliyah says, *"Bye, Graham Cracker."*

Graham Cracker says, *"Bye, Aaliyah. Pick you up tomorrow night at 10:00 p.m. sharp."* Aaliyah hears him clearly. To everyone else, it sounds like, *"Woof woof woof."* Graham Cracker sits in the doorway as Aaliyah and her mom drive off... *"Bye..."*

CHAPTER SIX

Finalizing the Plan

The next morning, Aaliyah wakes up to *"Rise and shine, sunshine."* She grins. She loves hearing her mom's cheery voice.

"Always starts the day off right," she thinks, smiling from ear to ear. She puts her slippers on and makes her way to the kitchen table. Lucky Charms and milk with a glass of apple juice. Armani has a bowl of Cinnamon Toast Crunch with milk and bottled water. She is dressed, her teeth are brushed, and she is in the car by 7:30 a.m., backpack in hand.

School seems long today. Aaliyah keeps thinking about the plan. *"We have to keep Dark Madness from putting our lights out... we need colour, sunshine, blue skies. Dark Madness would be leaving us in a dark hole of despair and loneliness, and sooner than later, worse... death."* Aaliyah looks up at the clock. *"1:59 p.m.,"* she mumbles to herself. *"Oh, good, only 10 minutes left."* The school bell rings every day at 2:09 p.m. Aaliyah, with a slight head tilt and brow crunch, wonders, *"That's an odd time. Why not just 2:10, an even number? Why do we find it odd, to end in odd... hmmmmm..."* She ponders for a minute or two, and then the bell rings. She is glad to be out of school, even if she has to wait until 10:00 p.m. Trying to stay focused during math

35

class is hard enough, but while distracted, well, that's just totally impossible.

Armani attends the middle school. He gets to the bus stop 10 minutes before Aaliyah's bus arrives. He waits for her to arrive, and then they walk home together. They only live five houses down, but Mom and Dad feel better when Armani walks his younger sister home. Mom usually gets home 10 minutes after them, but on rare occasions she is home before them. That doesn't happen often, but she is never more than 10 minutes after them.

Armani asks, *"Lots of homework?"* He looks over his shoulder, down at Aaliyah.

Aaliyah says, *"Some. I'm gonna do it right away, get it over with. It's math; I'm not a fan."*

Armani chuckles. *"It's not just you who isn't a fan of math."*

Aaliyah, knowing she has a busy night ahead of her, gets her homework completely done. Sitting at her desk, she thinks, *"Ahhh, one thing done."* Taking the trash out normally needs prompting, but today, she handles all her chores immediately. After everything is done, she showers and puts on some fresh pyjamas.

Mom says, *"Come here, child, let me feel your forehead. You feeling okay? Better yet, who has my child? I want her back!"* Sarah chuckles.

Aaliyah says, *"Mommmmmmmmm…"* with a shy grin. She blushes. Both of them stand there laughing.

Mom says, *"Dinner will be ready in five minutes."*

Aaliyah, looking over at the stove, knows what they are having. *"Okay,"* she calls out. *"Yummmm,"* she mumbles, *"fried chicken, rice and beans, and Brussels sprouts."* She cleans her desk and collects her homework and places it all in her backpack. *"It will be easier in the morning if everything is set in place tonight."* Aaliyah mumbles to herself, *"Just in case I am tired in the morning."* She wasn't tired the last time she was in the Mystical Forest for hours, but it really wasn't hours. *"Time is so weird there,"* she thinks. It's hard to understand, never mind trying to explain it. After cleaning up, she runs into the kitchen.

Mom says, *"No running!"*

Aaliyah says, *"Sorry."*

Mom says, *"Dinner is ready; did you wash your hands?"*

Aaliyah had dumped her pencil sharpener. In cleaning up the pencil shavings, her hands had gotten full of soot. After cleaning her desk, she washed her hands. *"Yes, Mom,"* she responds, *"I did."*

Mom says, *"Good, then let's eat."*

They all sit down for dinner. They are all busy eating with lips smacking, teeth chewing, and lots of *"mmmmmm"* sounds.

Mom says, *"Dinner must be good, or you were all just famished. No talking, but a lot of mmmmmmm going on."* Mom smiles with a sense of confidence and accomplishment. She always feels good when her family is happy.

Dad says with a chuckle, *"Everything is wonderful; thank you for your hard work. You must have slaved over the stove half the day."*

Mom says, *"No. At least a couple of hours, but you're all worth it."* Mom smiles and winks in the direction of Armani and Aaliyah.

Aaliyah thinks 10:00 p.m. will never get here. She has left her window cracked, just like she did for Lilly. She giggles. How a 103-pound goldendoodle is going to pass through a crack, well, that is too much for her to think about right now. *"Well, I'm going to bed early so that I will be alert for our meeting,"* she thinks to herself.

Graham Cracker says, *"I'm here."*

Aaliyah, spinning to her side, says, *"Wow, how?"* Quickly, she says, *"Never mind; we gotta go. Lots to do."*

Graham Cracker says, *"Jump on."*

Aaliyah says, *"Jump on?"*

Graham Cracker says, *"Yes, get on my back. You will see."*

Off they go. Graham Cracker, being a trained transporter, is able to travel Aaliyah back and forth to Mystical Forest. Puff... poof... out comes Graham Cracker. Puff... poof... Aaliyah makes it through. Somehow, even though she is riding Graham Cracker, they get separated and enter the portal separately. Ironically, it is still light out. Aaliyah, when she thinks of time and how it works, has the same response, she shakes her head from side to side.

Abby is waiting for them at the transport station. Graham Cracker is picked up by the nice lady Michelle from the transport school. Michelle says, *"Hi, I'm here to bring you back to the Morgan-Rizzo Transport School for extra powers they decided would be useful."* Amanda enjoys working with Graham Cracker and has thought of some ideas that may further help in their attack against Dark Madness.

Aaliyah jumps onto Abby's back. She immediately turns towards the Hubble, where they are to meet.

Abby says, *"Ready for takeoff."* Up and over they go, just as she had experienced with Graham Cracker. It is all new to her. Aaliyah thinks it is so cool to be flying in the air on a flying dog or unicorn. How many girls could say that? Her mind is wandering, but she catches herself... *"I must stay focused; important work is ahead. But I'm flying, really flying."*

Abby says, *"Here you go, Aaliyah. Safe and sound at the Hubble. I'll see you shortly. I'll be back."* Abby flaps her wings like she is waving. She is so beautiful in the air as her pink hair blows in the wind with her colourful horn and wings. She is breathtaking; no other words can describe the view of Abby in the sky in all her beauty and glory. She is happy; she is free. Free to fly, speak, breathe. Once Aaliyah's favourite toy, now her companion in the fight of their lives, for everyone's lives. If they don't win, if they don't conquer Dark Madness, everyone's fate will undoubtedly be bleak, and they will face certain doom. Aaliyah turns and makes her way into the Hubble. Inside, Lilly and Aizen are already there at work, discussing the latest intel. A few others were asked to be present. Joshua, head of the authorities, is one of them. He has the power to see bad intentions. When he sees bad intentions, he tries to derail and change the outcome of a situation. Jill, head of education and languages, is able to communicate to a great number of the population. Let's not forget being able to understand intel coming from different languages. They speak many, but she makes it her job to know all dialects. She is their best chance at communicating to all homes in Mystical Forest. She can also decipher intel that may come in through more sophisticated codes. She's proven very useful in the past. They need all the help they could get. *"All hands on deck,"* as they say on Earth.

Lilly explains, *"Dark Madness is one of the strongest sorcerers we have seen to date, and it is imperative we succeed, or we will be eliminated... forever."*

Then there is Rosko. He is an interesting fellow. He looks wise, he has spots, and he also has a deep voice. He is older, but still very good-looking and strong in structure. He is the commander of the army. Albeit they are a peaceful community, they're always prepared to fight evil when they are faced with it. Lastly, Tristan is sitting at the head of the table. They all seem to address him. He is the one who is going to run things from the Hubble and relay back to Aizen and Lilly out in the field.

After a couple minutes of introductions, Aizen says, *"Let's get started. We have compiled all the latest intel. On screen one, we have a picture of what Dark Madness looks like before and after morphing. Take a good, hard look,"* he says sharply.

Joshua says, *"All the criminal activities are leading to him. He is causing riots, breaking windows, smashing cars, and there is even rumour of a virus that may hit Earth. I believe it will be called Madness Gas."*

Rosko says, *"My men are ready, and they have received all of the special colour ray guns. They have improved the model. Once a ray gun shoots a protective coat over something, nothing can penetrate it. Not even Dark Madness will be able to. We have to lay this protective shield from one end of the Earth to the other before he enters. By laying the shield, the sorcerer will not be able to penetrate it with his evil gases. We must all execute our jobs perfectly, with no hesitation. Everything must go off precisely the way we have planned. It's imperative."*

Jill says, *"Yes, sir. I have prepared a very detailed correspondence that will be hand-delivered to everyone in Mystical Forest."*

Lilly says, *"Looks like we are ready."*

Aizen says, *"Let's do this!"* as he slams his fist on the table.

Aaliyah says, *"Let's get this sorcerer."*

Tristan says, *"I will remain here for the duration. I will be keeping all communication channels open. Everyone should be reporting back to me hourly. The girls from the Morgan-Rizzo Transport School will be manning the telecommunications. Therefore, I will be able to process the intel quickly."*

Lilly says to Aaliyah, *"It's time for you and Graham Cracker to go back home. Soon, we will start with phase 1."*

Aaliyah asks, *"How many phases are there?"*

Lilly answers, *"Five in total."*

Aaliyah nods, turns to Abby, and jumps onto her back. *"See you later, Lilly."*

Lilly says, *"Bye."*

Aaliyah jumps off Abby and hops on Graham Cracker for the remainder of the ride home, because Abby will be staying. Abby is staying in Mystical Forest at the Morgan-Rizzo Transport School. Samantha has grown fond of her and enjoys working with her and showing her as much as she can.

"Thanks for the ride, Abby. I'll miss you. Love you." Aaliyah is happy for her, but she is worried. When this is done, if they champion their fight against the evil sorcerer, will Abby be able to return to the Mystical Forest? There is no time to ponder that too hard now; there is far too much to do.

Graham Cracker enters the portal with Aaliyah on his back. *"Back to Earth,"* Graham Cracker barks out. They quickly reach her bedroom.

"Thanks, Graham Cracker," Aaliyah says as she hops off.

Graham Cracker says, *"I gotta go, Aaliyah. See you later. Love you."*

Aaliyah says, *"Goodnight; love you too."*

She goes out like a light, as they say. Aaliyah is tuckered out from all the night's activities; they wore her down. Fast asleep. Off to dreamland... zzzzzzzz...

CHAPTER SEVEN

Execution of the Phases: Protecting Planet Earth

They had agreed to meet the next evening at 9:00 p.m. to execute their plan. A special colour ray blaster was sized for a harness while they were there, and now it is being finalized. It will be strapped to both sides of Graham Cracker so that when he flies, he can spread a shield of colour to protect the people of Earth. Two huge sheets of the colour shield will express out the ray guns. This non-penetrating colour shield should prove to be stronger than the powers of Dark Madness. Although his powers are very strong, the fairies have worked very hard to find a non-penetrating material. Just a month ago, they were successful in doing just that. So they hope, anyways. They have to be conscientious about it, for if they miss a spot, well...

Rosko and the armies are out in full force. They are covering the Earth using their new and improved colour ray guns. Rosko and his troops are quite the strong, fierce-looking force. Literally thousands make up his army, and his success rate is very, very good with next to no casualties.

Jill has already sent out all the letters to the school children's parents. Furthermore, correspondence has been sent out to every local and not-so-local businesses. For all remaining citizens, a letter has been hand-delivered to their very homes. The letter instructs them as to what their role is in the execution of the plan to defeat Dark Madness. The letter states:

Dear people of Mystical Forest,

As you know, we have been awaiting the attack on us by Dark Madness. We have been developing equipment that will best protect us in this dark time. Dark Madness is one of the most powerful sorcerers we have had to face. That being said, we feel confident in our plan and our new and improved equipment. This evening, please go to your set community barn and you will all receive your new colour ray guns. They are safe to use around your children. I have received many emails referencing the safety of being hit by the colour ray. The rays serve as protection against evil. The evil component cannot penetrate the layer of protective colour shield, but you can splash each other and all will be fine. That being said, you are to spray all around your homes and neighbourhoods. Refills will be provided at the community barn at all hours. Someone will be posted at that spot every 24 hours until the threat is no longer. Once your homes and neighbourhoods are completely sprayed, make your way to the portals and start spraying Planet Earth. It will require all to participate fully if this plan is to roll out without any hitches. Any further questions, feel free to contact me.

Thank you,

Jill
Head of Communications and Languages

"Everyone in Mystical Forest has a role; that's the only way this is gonna work," Aaliyah thinks aloud. She is running through the plan in her head.

Joshua has his best men out and he has some staying nearby, as Mystical Forest is definitely going to be a hot zone. If Dark Madness wipes them out, well, there won't be a contest at all. Everything would sadly die.

Tristan and the girls of the Morgan-Rizzo Transport School will be remaining in the Hubble.

"Everything's ready to go!" Aaliyah yells. They have gathered in the woods behind Grandma's house. Ironically, at this spot where they all first met, they will attempt to conquer the most formidable opponent to date. They are about to get on with their plan.

They are starting with Rhode Island, the smallest of all the states. They will be laying the protective colours by foot, sky, and don't forget sea. Oh yeah, we haven't talked much about the gilled fairies. They are called Trites, you know, after King Triton and the mermaid people. The Trites have a very strong army as well. Aaliyah is riding Abby. Graham Cracker, carrying a uniquely-created colour ray blaster that can spread double the amounts at a faster speed, is ready to go. *"Go Abby, go!"* yells Aaliyah. In the air they go, Graham Cracker behind her. *"Wow, what a beautiful sight: the rainbows are flowing in the air like a carpet. This is better, though, more like a blanket, yes, the very best, your favourite, perhaps, draping you in comfort and protection."* They keep moving. Everyone is doing what they are supposed to. They are staying organized. Rhode Island, Massachusetts, Connecticut, New York...

Beep Beep Beep intel coming in. Tristan is alerting Aaliyah on her telecommunication device. With the hit of a button, Tristan appears on the screen. *"Beware, Dark Madness is in New York. We just received information of a sighting. He is in the area of the Statue of Liberty."* Moving fast to shield the area, Aaliyah and Abby pick up speed and head right over in that direction. Time is of the most importance; they must beat the sorcerer and get the protective shield up before Dark Madness makes his moves to finish them. Graham Cracker has circled around the other way and will meet Aaliyah at the Liberty statue. They have timed it so that they will reach the target at about the same time. *"Let's go, Abby; we must hurry if we are to beat him,"* Aaliyah exclaims nervously, but she is determined to succeed. She has worked hard on the plan. With all their training, it just has to work! *"If he gets there before us, I don't know what could happen. Don't want to find out either,"* she says as she pats Abby on the hip that bears her heart-shaped marking. *"Let's Gooo!"* she says while continuing to spray the beautiful colour shield throughout the city.

"We finally made it. I see the Statue of Liberty just up ahead. There's the Liberty girl," Abby calls out.

Aaliyah says, "Wow, what a view. The Twin Towers were somewhere not far from here as well. I learned about it in history class. It's known as 9/11. It's a big piece of history. Sadly, the Towers were struck down by an evil villain of Earth. A guy named Bin Laden, I think, something like that. He had people drive planes through the buildings where people worked. The buildings were long and lean, and they ran up into the sky, just like the long legs of the 'Radio City Dancers,' always in sync. The Dancers were best known for their performances at the Radio City Music Hall in Manhattan, New York. New York is the home of many entertainment celebrities, singers, and actors as well as theatre. It was sad and scary time, that dreaded day, September 11th, 2001. Things would never be the same again. We must stay focused so that we are triumphant." They started spraying, making their way up and all around the statue and area. Lilly rides near Graham Cracker's ear for protection until they all meet at the top of the statue.

"Our job is done here. Either we got lucky, or he has decided to attack another area. Let's keep moving; we want to get ahead of him," Lilly cries out.

New Jersey, Delaware, Maryland, Washington DC...

Beep beep beep... *"Wait, it's Tristan; he's coming through the telecommunication device,"* Lilly says emphatically. Tristan appears. *"Yes, Tristan, any new news?"*

Tristan says, *"Yes, Lilly, there seems to be chaos near the White House and capital area. We believe there is a riot beginning. It's escalating into pure mayhem. You must get there before the area becomes totally out of control and they destroy each other, never mind the sorcerer's handiwork. Or maybe that's his objective: cause complete craziness and the people hurt each other. This would leave Dark Madness sitting back and watching, while the people of Earth destroy each other. Nevertheless, may the force be with you, and carry on..."* Tristan is out, just like that.

Lilly says, *"Let's go; no time to waste."*

They are streaming down along the Potomac River, looking at its neoclassical monuments and buildings. You know, Greek-looking, tall pillars, columns, plain blank walls... the simplicity makes it grand in its stature. There are many iconic museums, and performing arts venues, oh yeah, and let's not forget the Space Center... Kennedy Space Center. Okay, and back to the story, enough with the history lesson. They see the rioting taking place. They are in disbelief that this much commotion is taking place in the wee hours when people should be sleeping. This is a crazy thing to see. They spray their colourful rays and they can see a change in the air. It is becoming calmer.

Aaliyah says, *"Well, it's one of two things. One, people are getting tired and the rowdy behaviour is slowing down; or two, the colour rays do really calm and protect once it is covered, like a mom wrapping her warm arms around a child and rocking them to sleep, nice and safe. I hope it's two, so that once we move on, this area will be considered protected."*

Virginia, Ohio, Indiana, Iowa... all the troops keep on marching.

Beep beep beep...

"It's Tristan," Lilly says to Aaliyah. *"Yes, Tristan, what's the latest?"*

Tristan says, *"It seems he hit New York, but you had already secured the areas. He was unable to penetrate the colour rays you shielded the city with. That's great news; we now are 100% certain that our new and improved equipment is working. Keep up the great work. You have managed to get ahead of him and stop him at his own game. Great work!"*

Aaliyah says, *"Wow, that's great news, and a relief. But there is so much left to do. So many states."*

Graham Cracker says, *"Glad we saved New York and calmed Washington down."*

Aaliyah says, *"That's for sure!"*

As they continue out of Washington D.C., they look back and notice that the evil is rising above the rainbow-coloured layer. It is like it is being squeezed out of the coloured bands that have formed the shield. It is beautiful yet eerie. The layer above has a sinister look as well as feel. It is spooky. It is like what you think of at Halloween, the weird scary sky to drive your senses to a scary, chilling place... As they pull farther away, they continue to see streams of colour bursting through the dark heavy film. Aaliyah thinks, *"We must keep moving; no time to be spectators. All is good here."* On they go.

CHAPTER EIGHT

The First Head-to-Head Encounter

They have been at this for hours now, or so it feels. The whole time difference is so hard to follow. Mystical Forest time versus Earth time. So confusing!

"Big lights. It's nighttime, but with so many lights and so many people up, how could it be nighttime here?" asks Aaliyah. She reads the sign: *"Welcome to Las Vegas."*

Graham Cracker is looking all around. *"WOWSIE, this place is cool. Talk about lights,"* he says with his eyes wide. *"May need sunglasses here, even at night."* The billboards are all lined up, one right after another, advertising the headliner shows, you know, the hired entertainment for the evening.

Lilly says, *"Let's start in the communities. If we blanket the communities first, we can protect the locals and then make our way to the vacationers, or the young people attending a concert of their favourite groups, or a boxing match."*

Abby moves swiftly towards the residential areas, you know, where the locals sleep, with Aaliyah riding on her back. Aaliyah has mastered shifting her body with Abby's. It makes it easier for them to get speed. Aaliyah is no longer nervous. She has grown used to travelling on Abby and never fears falling off. Graham

Cracker and Lilly follow as they make their way to the individual communities.

Aaliyah calls out, *"We are heading to this side; you keep going that way. We will meet on the strip."*

Graham Cracker says, *"Okay, see you soon."* Off they continue.

Aaliyah reaches old Vegas, Golden Nugget, Fremont Street Experience, Mob Museum, then Heart Attack Grill. Aaliyah chuckles. *"Must be one heck of a burger to give you a heart attack."* She reads the sign. *"They use a whole pound of beef, and not the 86% fat-free. Not the organic, grass-fed burger my grandma uses. Looks good, though, even in the picture. Slot machines, Zilla Zipline. Hmmmmm, now that looks like fun."* Farther up, she hits the new Vegas strip. Stratosphere, Sahara, Circus Circus, Wynn, Treasure Island. Aaliyah says, *"I can't believe how cool this place is. Everything looks fun. The lights are bright; no one looks tired."* The Venetian, The Flamingo, Caesars Palace, Planet Hollywood. All are equally spectacular, yet each of the resorts has its own style. She passes by as they spray the colourful protective shield. As she gets farther down the strip, she spots a darkening sky. *"Abby, look ahead; looks like trouble. The sky seems to really be darkening."* Aaliyah taps Abby on the heart-marking, *"Let's go; we must hurry. There's trouble ahead."*

Lilly, not knowing if Aaliyah notices the darkening sky, says, *"Look ahead."*

Aaliyah turns and notices Graham Cracker coming up behind her. Aaliyah says, *"What should we do?"*

Lilly says, *"Let's spray as we move towards the darkness, but let's remain together."*

Aaliyah says, *"Sounds good to me."*

They pass Aria, Walgreens, MGM, Excalibur.

Aaliyah says, *"Looks like it's over by New York, New York. OMG, here we go again. It's New York Resort in Las Vegas. How crazy. We almost met up in New York City; now, we are at the resort but in Vegas."* Aaliyah continues, *"The people on the roller coaster are in trouble!"*

Lilly and Graham Cracker rush on over there. Lilly says, *"Something isn't right... it's sooo DARK!"*

When they get there, the roller coaster, also known as the 'Big Apple Coaster,' is emerged in thick, dark, wet-feeling air. The air is sinister-looking. It looks as though the people are not yelling in cheer but in fear. In an instant, it looks like a total blackout. People are screaming; the man who was operating the machine has passed out. The coaster, not being manned, begins to speed up and up and up. People are beginning to run for safety. The winds begin blowing so quickly and forcibly. Dust, sand, papers that had been dropped, and trash cans are whirling around, emptying in the night air that is now sticky, wet, and dirty, adding to the confusion taking place. They approach carefully. It is so dark that seeing is almost impossible, but they can hear the wind circling around. They don't want to be caught up in it.

Lilly yells, *"Be careful. We can't help anyone if something happens to us."*

Aaliyah throws a thumbs up. Despite the darkness, Lilly is able to see Aaliyah's gesture. Graham Cracker decides to go up higher to see if he can get a view of the darkness where it may have started, or stopped. He wants to see how high it has reached. Mostly, he wants to check for any signs of Dark Madness.

Lilly says, *"Down there, over by the Luxor sign, Mandalay Bay Resorts."*

Graham Cracker swoops down to beat the sinister sorcerer, quickly spreading the protective cover of light over the area. Once again, they can see the lights pushing the darkness out and through the bands of light.

Lilly says, *"Phew, that was close."*

As they turn, they see that Aaliyah and Abby are still trying to protect the people over by the coaster. Lilly, catching up to Aaliyah, says, *"I contacted Aizen; he's sending reinforcements."*

Moments later, Aizen appears. Aizen says, *"Hey, I'm here; we got this."* He has a special vacuum-type gadget. The vacuum begins sucking the dust and debris from the dark sky. At least they aren't being hit by flying debris any longer. A trash can had been whisked up into the air, almost knocking Aaliyah off Abigail at one point. People begin to drop to the ground, out cold, sleeping.

"How is this happening?" Aaliyah cries out...

Aizen says, "It's gas, sleeping gas swirling in the air with the dust particles. We must work faster if we are to win this battle. Right now, he has the edge on us!"

Aaliyah says, "Oh no, we must prevail, we must."

Aizen says, "The foot soldiers and I will keep moving ahead; we will get ahead of him. If we can get the colour shield to spread before he is able to totally penetrate the area with his darkness, we should be okay. He just seems to be picking up speed though."

Aizen and the footmen move on, pressing forward and making good gains. Meanwhile, Aaliyah and Abby have their hands full. The Big Apple Coaster has come unconnected from the high winds and obviously Dark Madness's handiwork. A couple of the cable cars are barely hanging. Now, the people hanging upside down are screaming even more loudly. Will they plunge to their deaths? At this moment it is unknown, but Abby and Aaliyah work hard to free the people from their cable cars and return them to a safe spot. The spectators cannot see that it is a giant beautiful unicorn and a little girl on its back who are saving them. Never mind a flying dog with a fairy. Nevertheless, that's just what is happening. Aaliyah and the gang have finally returned all the participants of the ride to a safe place.

The people, as they are rescued, begin to talk. "Did you see a unicorn?"

"I saw a flying dog and a winged girl."

"Has the stress of what we just went through affected our ability to process what has happened?"

"Are we in a dream state? Are we really alive? Or did we pass over and that's how we are seeing mystical-type creatures?" Mumbles in the small group continue...

One man says to a spectator, *"Did you see anything strange? Did you by chance see who rescued us?"*

The spectator says, *"No, sorry, the smog is so thick that up until now we couldn't even see our feet. It's just starting to lift now."*

Aaliyah says, *"We must keep pressing forward and catch up to Aizen. This was too close. Dark Madness almost got us this time."*

Lilly says, *"But he didn't. Great job, everyone."*

Off they go, spraying the sky with the beautiful colourful streams of that wonderfully-protective shield. Medicine that protects you from ailments usually tastes awful. This protection, well, is different. It is so beautiful. The people of Earth have no clue just how this beautiful scene is actual protection. They think it means a warm day is coming. They think it is a beautiful ending to a good weather day. A rainbow after a storm. Aaliyah's mind drifts for a moment... *"When I see rainbows after a rainstorm, is that a protective shield? Did I just not realize it before now?"*

Graham Cracker says, *"Come on, Aaliyah, catch up."*

Aaliyah says, *"Abby, let's go!"*

The four ride through the night sky with a trail of colour falling behind them as they continue moving forward. Aizen and the footmen make great gains as well. They keep going. Arizona, Colorado, California...

CHAPTER NINE

Disney is Under Attack

B eep beep beep... more intel coming in...

The Morgan-Rizzo girls realize that Aizen is wrapping things up in Las Vegas with some of Rosko's footmen.

Samantha says, *"What are we going to do? Aizen isn't here."*

Tristan says, *"Retrieve the intel. Once we know what exactly is happening, we can figure out our next move."*

...Dark Madness is approaching Florida's Disney World...

Vanessa speaks out, *"That's a high tourist area and on the opposite side of where they are all at now. Disneyland is in California, but Dark Madness is playing it smart. He moved fast to the other side of the country."*

Amanda says, *"Thank goodness for portals. What's good for Dark Madness works for us too!"*

Samantha says, *"That's right. Let's get the rest of the intel and get everyone set up to beat this monster sorcerer once and for all."*

...Dark Madness is nearing Florida's Disney World area, Orlando, Kissimmee... lots of residential communities as well as vacation spots and parks...

Lilly says, *"Aaliyah, I just received word that Dark Madness is quickly approaching Florida."*

They rush on, using every portal they can. They know they have to reach Florida as fast as they can fly.

Graham Cracker says, *"WOWSIE! It's so dark here, just like in Las Vegas, near New York Resort. Boy oh boy oh boy, we're in for another fight."*

Lilly says, *"We can do this; stay positive! We need to go low, under the darkness. This will keep some protection closer to the people and hopefully, like in the past, it will push the dark, sticky, and, in this case, smelly smog out."*

Aaliyah says, *"We're going to need help. We can't be everywhere at once, and Florida, with all its attractions, well, there is a lot of land to cover. There's Universal Studios, Disney Springs, Animal Kingdom, Hollywood Studios, Sea World, Dolphin Discovery Cove, Gatorland, that's just to name a few. How can we win?"* She cries out in the voice of a girl who is young, tired, and beaten, *"How?"* A tear runs down her very tired, scared face. She knows how important it is to defeat the sorcerer, or all will soon be gone, died off, extinct.

Lilly says, *"Don't give up now, Aaliyah; don't lose hope now. We got this! The Morgan-Rizzo girls are on their way on their personally-trained mystical pets."*

The Morgan-Rizzo girls immediately head out. Amanda is on a mystical cat, Midnight. She has witchery-type powers that can change things at a moment's notice. Most times, she is able to change potential bad outcomes. Vanessa is on her white tiger, Kora. She has one of the specially-made double-sided ray blasters, like what Graham Cracker was sized for. Samantha is on her magnificent dragon, Peaches. Her powers are, well, crazy, with fire-breath shooting out when faced with evildoers. In this case, Peaches can spray colourful rays that produce the same protective shield as the ray guns.

Aaliyah says, *"Oh, thank goodness; the more help we can get, the better."*

As they start into the park, the girls on their amazingly trained and powerful pets come up behind them.

Amanda asks, *"Where should we start?"*

Lilly says, *"Head over to Universal Studios, then Hollywood Studios. Graham Cracker and I will head over to Animal Kingdom. Aaliyah, you and Abby handle Magic Kingdom. I noticed Rosko and his footmen are at Disney Springs."*

Aaliyah asks, *"What about all the other parks? There are so many."*

Lilly says, *"Aizen just finished up in Las Vegas. He and the footmen with him are using the portals to get here as quickly as they can. They will communicate with me so that I can let them know of our progress and where we most need them upon their arrival."*

Aaliyah says, *"Great! No time to spare chit-chatting. Let's go, Abby."*

Aaliyah and Abby enter Disney World's Magic Kingdom and head towards Main Street USA. They spray the protective colour shield down low but high enough so that the dark smog coming their way cannot get past the shield. Harm cannot reach the patrons. As they blow by town square, they shield all the small restaurants, bakeries, ice cream parlors, coffee shops, and Cinderella's Castle, where the Disney characters dine with the visitors.

Aaliyah says, *"Abby, go that way, through Adventureland."*

They move swiftly past Tinkerbell's Magic Nook, Swiss Family Robinson treehouse, Enchanted Tiki Room, Jungle Cruise, and Pirates of the Caribbean.

"OMG," Aaliyah calls out, *"are those pirates shooting at us?"*

Abby says, *"Get your ray gun ready and hold on."*

Abby skillfully swoons in. Although her powers are new to her, she is very confident she can handle anything she is faced with. Abby realized the importance of keeping Aaliyah safe and the importance of saving her girl, Aaliyah. They have been best friends for years, and now Abby is able to be a vital part of saving the world and her best friend who she loves more than anyone else. Aaliyah has her ray gun ready... ssssssssssss... ssssssssssss... This is the sound it makes as it expels the beautiful shades of colour. The protective shield has proven strong enough to hold back Dark Madness in New York and again in Las Vegas. Sssssssssss... Abby swoops over to the other side, then the other. Aaliyah is pretty good at hitting all her targets as well, all while shifting her body to move with Abby's swooping.

Aaliyah says, *"Oh no, what was that? Looks like a giant black fireball. A large lump of coal on fire."*

Abby swoops, ducking the fireballs that are heading towards them. It seems they are under attack. No time to be fearful; they have a mission to complete.

Aaliyah cries out, *"The evil sorcerer must be stopped!"*

The battle continues for some time. They battle the Pirates of the Caribbean for what seems like hours until the colour ray guns' rays freeze them. The pirates look like marble statues. They are turned into stone. There is no time to figure out why. They move on. Frontierland, Liberty Square, Fantasyland, and then Tomorrowland.

Meanwhile, over at Universal Studios, Samantha, one of the Morgan-Rizzo girls, is knocked off her mystical dragon, Peaches. She is a beautiful white dragon with colourful wings and a bright coral stripe running down her chest. She is stunning both in her stature, size, and beauty. Peaches makes a downward dive and grabs Samantha from the air, carefully bringing her down to where a slightly shaken girl can regain a comfortable position. Back in the saddle, so they say. Samantha gets back up on Peaches.

"Let's go," Samantha calls out. *"Now I'm mad! What the heck was that?"*

Vanessa says, *"It was a wizard."*

The evil wizard calls out, *"I am Abaddon."* His name in Hebrew means ruin, destruction. Abaddon and Ambrose, another dark wizard, are shooting fireballs with their wizard staffs. The staff is a power conduit tool. There are different levels of power a staff holds. Samantha had been under attack when she ducked hard, causing her to lose her balance and fall off of Peaches. Amanda and Vanessa on their mystical creatures come in rapidly to aid in controlling the wizards. The evil is no match for the colour ray guns. The battle goes on for some time. The girls are triumphant and move on to Hollywood Studios. Luckily for them, having just endured a tough battle in the wooded area where some of the toughest Wizards known in Black Alley live, Rosko and his foot soldiers are also entering Hollywood Studios.

Amanda says, *"Glad you're all here; we just fought for our lives. Glad to see we have numbers at this point. We need as much help as we can get."*

Lilly and Graham Cracker are encountering their own kind of troubles. If you remember, they were headed over to Animal Kingdom. When they reach the park, the animals are angry, agitated. The dinosaurs over at the Avatar attraction are moving towards them.

Lilly says, *"So much for statues and a friendly tour of the wild calm animals in their habitats."*

The Yeti is stomping down Forbidden Mountain.

Lilly says, *"Oh my, Graham Cracker, we are gonna have to really get moving here. Looks like Dark Madness has disturbed the animals. They almost all look possessed, evil."*

Graham Cracker has to bob and weave. On one side he has the dinosaurs in the air, trying to swat at him. Lilly hangs on for dear life. She has tucked herself into Graham Cracker's ear for protection. Remember Lilly is a very, very little fairy. Graham Cracker is moving so fast she could barely hang on. On the other side, he is being charged at by the Yeti. A Yeti is, in Himalayan folklore, a monstrous creature. Over time, it has become better known as the Abominable Snowman. Graham Cracker is proving to be fast. Although his opponents are big, very big, strong, and scary, they are no match for his speed and agility. Graham Cracker shows no sign of fear, and he is definitely proving to be inexhaustible. He is like the Energizer Bunny: he keeps going and going. He is not like the generic, cheap kind of battery. While fighting the creatures off, he continues to spray sheets of protective colours from his specially-made double-barrel ray blaster.

Graham Cracker says, *"What will become of the animals? They have obviously turned evil; they're infected."* Graham is sombre. He has an idea from past encounters of what will become of them.

"Statues," Lilly says in a low voice. *"They must be turned into statues, or they will continue to create chaos and ultimately win."*

You see, that's the sad thing about evil. Once you are evil, it's almost impossible to go back to just being good. This brings us to Daryl, otherwise known as Dark Madness: the evil sorcerer. At one time, he was a warm, loving man. That's why so many of the Mystical Forest creatures become sad when they speak of Dark Madness. They know they must beat him, but they don't like the idea.

Lilly says, *"We must head over to Dolphin Discovery Cove and Sea World. King Triton and the Trites are already working the waters there."*

Joshua and the municipality have joined them. Originally, Joshua, Head of Criminal Investigation and everything in that nature, was to stay in Mystical Forest. But things are under control at the moment, and Planet Earth needs reinforcements. Tristan is back in the Hubble with the nice lady Michelle from the Morgan-Rizzo Transport School. She had gone over to help when Samantha, Amanda, and Vanessa transported to help with their own pets. When they arrive, Joshua and his men are present, as are Rosko and his footmen. Aaliyah is on Abby; Samantha, Amanda, and Vanessa are on their pets; and here comes Graham Cracker and Lilly. There is no sign of Aizen; he must be off fighting evil.

Vanessa asks, *"Anyone see Dark Madness?"*

Everyone mumbles *"NO!"*

Aaliyah says, *"I'm gonna head to Dolphin Discovery Cove; you guys handle Sea World and the local communities on this side."*

They all head in their proper directions, knocking out as much territory as they can in a short time. When Aaliyah reaches the park, she notices that the dolphins are jumping erratically. And the water itself is bumpy, angry, with a definite sinister feeling. It is dark, and it looks like the black cloak of a wizard is pounding the water's surface, causing waves. That is odd because these waters are man-made and calm, with no waves. But that is not the case tonight. It is unnerving.

King Triton and the Trites send help to calm the waters there. Remember these fairies with gills? They are trying to calm the waters from their violent waves.

Aaliyah says, *"Abby, do you see that?"*

Abby says *"Yes"* as she swallows down hard.

Their eyes and heads shift, automatically looking up at a massive image of a man in all black, growing in size.

"Oh my," Aaliyah cries. *"Nothing could have prepared me for this."* Aaliyah, swallowing her fear, proceeds to shoot her colour ray gun. She comments, *"It doesn't seem to be having much of an effect on him."*

Abby moves side to side and down and then back up. She thinks if she moves around, it may throw the sorcerer off and give Aaliyah an edge.

Aaliyah says, *"I don't think I can fight him; he is too big and strong."* She strains to hold the ray gun on him.

The sea creatures continue to stir, becoming even more aggressive and agitated. The sorcerer begins shooting fire balls at them. He is aiming for Aaliyah, figuring she must be in charge. After all, she is riding a creature. Abby continues to move quickly, never staying in any one spot for too long. Aaliyah, trying to remain calm, keeps her ray gun pointed at the huge figure. He is even larger and scarier than she had thought. At one point, they are close and she can feel an electric charge emanating from him. They move back as fast as they entered the space.

Aaliyah says, *"Wow, that hurt. Good thing we didn't go any closer. Abigail, make sure not to go too close; there must be an electrical field around him."*

Abby says, *"Roger that."*

The battle continues, but the single colour ray gun Aaliyah has is no match for the likes of Dark Madness's powers. Finally,

MONIQUE R LANDRY JOHNSON

the others make their way through and notice the thick smog infiltrating that area.

Lilly says, *"OMG, AALIYAH IS UNDER ATTACK. IT'S DARK MADNESS!"*

Everyone can now see what is happening. The girls move their heads in an upward motion, mouths open...

Amanda says, *"He's huge."*

The group quickly assembles in a circular formation, spraying the protective colour shield all over the Giant Dark Madness in his angry form.

DARK MADNESS SPEAKS: *"IF I CANNOT BE HAPPY, NO ONE CAN!"* He roars from the skies. He has grown so big, bigger than they had expected. He stands tall. *"NO ONE SHALL BE HAPPY!"*

The group continues to battle for hours. They definitely have a formidable villain on their hands. They are beginning to show signs of tiredness. All of a sudden, Aizen appears, flies right up and into Dark Madness's eye space, and looks the giant monster right in the eyes.

Aizen screams, *"DAD, STOP!"* He cries out as loudly as he has ever spoken. This takes everyone by surprise because they hadn't seen Aizen entering.

Aaliyah is amazed at his bravery, his act of courage. Her big golden eyes widen as she thinks about what she heard. *"Is Dark Madness Aizen's dad?"* she mumbles. She always knew Aizen was a frisky fellow, but to face the evilest villain and sorcerer to date; well, that's on some other level. She isn't easy to impress, but at this moment, Aizen impresses Aaliyah. Aaliyah is confused. *"I need to address that, that's for sure." Aaliyah* says. What Aaliyah needs to address is, how is Dark Madness Aizen's Dad. Why had he called out…. Dad?

Aizen says, *"STOP THIS NOW! WHY DO YOU WISH TO HURT US? GO AND LEAVE US TO OUR PEACEFUL WAYS. I WANT MY DAD BACK."*

Everyone remains still in amazement. They hadn't expected Aizen to appear from nowhere and immediately face the beast.

Aaliyah says, *"What's happening? Is that a tear coming from Dark Madness's eye?"* She shakes her head, feeling as though she must be mistaken. *"Wait, what... I'm so confused."*

All of a sudden, Dark Madness begins to shrink. He is no longer in the skies. Right before their eyes, he just vanishes, disappears... poof, he's gone! It is as though he is sucked through a black dark hole, probably the one he came through to invade Planet Earth in the first place.

Aaliyah calls out, *"How did he just disappear?"* Aaliyah is so confused.

The group, after holding their breath, lets out a sigh. It's over. They are all smiling, laughing, mumbling... it's over... finally over...

Lilly, confused herself, thinks, *"But maybe the spells we have been working on are starting to work. Dark Madness cowered down to Aizen. Did he recognize his son? Aizen did call out 'Dad.' That was a tear."* She mumbles to herself, eyes shifting while thinking. She taps her finger on her chin. *"Well, for now, anyways, we still have much work to do on with creating an altered spell that will break the curse of 'Green Eyes' and ultimately the prophecy,"* she says, knowing that she doesn't know when, where, or how, but he will be back. She wonders if the spells they are currently working on are beginning to work.

Aaliyah asks, *"Green Eyes?"*

Lilly says, *"I'll explain soon, but for now, let's go home and rest. Today was exhausting."*

CHAPTER TEN

The Battle has Ended

A aliyah says, *"I'm so tired."*

Graham Cracker says, *"Me too."*

The whole group mumbles in agreement. They all return to Mystical Forest. There are warm greetings and cheers upon their return. Aizen, Aaliyah notices, goes right to his home. She figures that's Aizen being Aizen. The Morgan-Rizzo girls are welcomed by their mom, Michelle. Rosko, Joshua, the Trites, the armies, and the footmen proceed to the community storage facility to store the ray guns and return to their homes as well.

Tristan says, *"Great job to you all!"*

Everyone is exhausted.

Aaliyah says, *"Time for me to head back before they notice I was gone."*

Graham Cracker says, *"Yeah, me too!"*

Aaliyah gives a big hug to Abby. *"I'll see you soon."* Aaliyah looks over at Lilly. *"I will... right? See you all again?"*

Lilly says, *"I will be by tomorrow, at your grandma's home."*

Graham Cracker and Aaliyah return back home through the portal. Aaliyah waves goodbye as they disappear. *"BYE."*

Everyone in Mystical Forest retires to their beds for what is left of the sleeping hours.

When Aaliyah and Graham Cracker return to Grandma's, Aaliyah is still full of questions but too tired to think of anything else for the evening. Aaliyah says, "Come, Graham Cracker, let's get some sleep. Tomorrow will be here before we know it."

CHAPTER ELEVEN

Meeting with Lilly, post-battle

(post: that means after)

Aaliyah, completely overwhelmed with all of the latest events and adventures, never stopped Lilly to ask her why. *"Why am I the chosen one? Why was I called on to save the world? Who else has powers? Will I see Abby again? Will Graham Cracker continue to speak the English language to me? Most of all, what is the whole Aizen situation? Is he my cousin? Is Dark Madness my uncle?"* She has so many unanswered questions. Lilly, before they headed back to Earth, had told Aaliyah she would be back to see her at her grandmother's house the next day.

Aaliyah and Graham Cracker wake up at their normal time.

Aaliyah says, *"Boy, as tired as we were, we still woke up at our usual time. It's crazy, but I don't feel like I lost any sleep either. I'll never get used to the time differences between Earth and Mystical Forest."*

Graham Cracker says *"I'm hungry, Aaliyah"* as he looks over to her, hoping she is just as eager to grab some grub. He says, *"I think I worked up a hearty appetite."*

The two go into the kitchen, where Grandma has prepared homemade waffles with all of the toppings... *"Yummmmm!"* Aaliyah exclaims. *"You're right, Graham Cracker; I'm famished as well."*

The two eat while Grandma cleans the kitchen. Then, Grandma sits at the table to sip her coffee while Aaliyah finishes breakfast.

Grandma says, *"What are you doing today, hunny? It's looking like a very dismal day outside."*

Aaliyah says, *"I was thinking of finishing my book and colouring a picture to go with the book report I need to do. Extra credit for pictures."*

Grandma says, *"Very good, my smart girl. I will knock on your door when lunch is ready. If you get tired of reading, I would be glad to play a game. No pressure, whatever works for you. Schoolwork is always more important!"*

Aaliyah says, *"Thanks for breakfast, Grandma. Awesome as usual. No Aunt Emily and Aizen today?"*

Grandma says, *"No they had something that they needed to finish at home. Just us today. You go on, get to that schoolwork. I'll clean up; there's plenty to keep me busy."*

Aaliyah and Graham Cracker head to the bedroom. Aaliyah sits at her desk after cracking open her window so Lilly can twinkle in. She pulls out her book. See, so it isn't completely a lie; she does intend to work on her book report while awaiting the arrival of Lilly. Once Lilly comes, well, then Aaliyah has so many questions to be answered. Graham Cracker is content just being near Aaliyah. He lies on the floor beside her desk. Aaliyah finishes reading her book. Now she is beginning her cover page.

Aaliyah asks, *"What did you think of the book?"* as she looks over at Graham Cracker.

Graham Cracker says, *"I like when you read to me. I like the sound of your voice."*

Aaliyah smiles. She enjoys the fact that Graham Cracker can talk. She is slightly concerned that he will go back to normal now that the mission is currently completed. She could deal with him going back to being an ordinary dog, but would she ever get to see

Abby again? Although if Abigail comes back, she would only be a stuffed toy. Now, she is a magnificent, beauteous creature. More important, Aaliyah has grown a stronger bond with Abby. After all, they just fought a raging battle during which time Aaliyah and Abigail had only each other for protection.

Aaliyah says, *"Hmmmmm, should I draw a unicorn?"*

Graham Cracker says, *"Sure... make her look like Abigail. She's real pretty."*

Aaliyah says, *"Wow, it's 12:30 p.m. already. I'm starting to feel hungry. Let's go see what Grandma is doing."*

They venture out of the bedroom. Grandma is sitting in her favourite chaise lounge, that's a fancy name for an oversized, comfy, TV-room chair. She is watching one of her shows from during the week. She sometimes records them, and she sometimes goes on demand. That's a feature some TV companies offer to watch a show that has previously played. It's a great feature if you ask me.

Aaliyah says, *"Hi, Grandma."*

Grandma says, *"Hi, princess. I have prepared lunch. I made a homemade soup, chicken, just like you like. I also prepared some grilled cheese sandwiches. I just have to heat them in the pan to warm the cheese."*

Aaliyah says, *"That sounds so good, and it's the perfect kinda day for soup too. Don't you think?"*

Grandma says, *"Yes, baby, you are right. That wind is howling like a grizzly bear that hasn't eaten in a month. Let's get into the kitchen before we start growling like the wind."* They go into the kitchen, while both laughing at the thought of their stomachs growling like grizzlies.

Aaliyah says, *"This is so good, Grandma. You always make my favourites."*

Grandma says, *"Well, that's easy, sweet girl. You like everything I make you. You're a good girl for Grandma. I love you."*

Aaliyah says, *"Awww, I love you too, Grandma."*

Graham Cracker says, *"I love you too, Aaliyah and Grandma."* Of course, to Grandma, it only sounds like Graham Cracker barking: *"Woof woof."*

Aaliyah helps Grandma clear the table and do the dishes. Aaliyah likes helping Grandma in the kitchen. They talk, laugh, and just love spending time together. They care very much for each other. Grandma loves pleasing Aaliyah with her favourite foods and a perfectly detailed room just for her. All her favourite things. The same goes for Armani, her brother. He also has a room designed with all his favourite things. Being older with his interests changing, that day is coming. You know, hanging out with friends and playing video games, or arranging a study date with a girl you think is cute. Yup, that day always comes, sadly. But, if the proper roots are formed in the early years, they will grow to be smart, responsible, thriving individuals.

Grandma asks, *"So, what are you planning on getting into now?"*

Aaliyah says, *"I was about to start my drawing for my book report."*

Grandma says, *"Oh nice, so you finished reading the book? Was it good?"* Grandma gave her a look. You know, that look you give when you are waiting for an answer.

Aaliyah says, *"Oh yes, very. I love reading about unicorns and mystical worlds. I can't wait to draw the unicorn for my cover page. She's gonna be beautiful. I can already picture her in my head."*

Grandma says, *"That is wonderful. Should make your job easy then."*

Grandma goes back to her chaise lounge. She is about to start a counted cross stitch pattern. She is looking up the floss numbers and will wind them on the thread spools. *"Let's see, hmmmmm... let's catch up on my Chicago shows,"* she mumbles to herself, *"Med, Fire, PD... Med first."*

She clicks the remote and begins spooling the floss.

Aaliyah and Graham Cracker go back into her room. Aaliyah immediately goes to her desk and begins drawing the most beautiful of beasts. Not a beast in what the name sounds like it signifies, but a large creature. An animal that is only in books on Planet Earth. Make-believe in the minds of human species.

At around 4:30 p.m., Grandma knocks on Aaliyah's door and says, *"Aaliyah."*

Aaliyah says, *"Come in."*

Grandma, walking in, moves towards Aaliyah at the desk. *"Wow, you weren't kidding."*

Aaliyah says, *"What do you mean, Grandma?"*

Grandma says, *"You said she was beautiful and you knew exactly how she looked, and she is! Kind of resembles your favourite stuffed unicorn up in the treehouse."*

Aaliyah smiles. *"Thanks, Grandma. Yes, she does."*

Grandma says, *"Are you hungry?"*

Aaliyah says, *"Not really much."*

Grandma says, *"Do you mean no, not really?"*

Aaliyah says *"Yes"* as she giggles. *"Okay, maybe some toast with soft butter and grape jam."*

Grandma says, *"That can be arranged... Coming right up!"* She heads off to the kitchen. Grandma, looking back at Aaliyah, says, *"Make sure you wash your hands. Been playing in those crayons all afternoon."*

Aaliyah says, *"Okay."*

After eating her toast, Aaliyah decides to take an early shower and hang out in the TV room for a bit. There is a Christmas special coming on. *Frosty the Snowman* is about to start. With a bowl of popcorn on their laps, Aaliyah and Grandma share the space on the chaise lounge. It is only a one-hour special and they have seen it before, but everyone enjoys watching TV specials every year. That's why they replay all the older ones as well as the newer shows throughout all of December.

Aaliyah says *"Goodnight, Grandma, love you!"* as she kisses her and moves off the chaise.

Grandma says, *"Goodnight, sweet dreams! Don't let the bed bugs bite."*

Smiling, Aaliyah brushes her teeth and off to her room she goes. Aaliyah knows Lilly is coming. She had said so, and Lilly never breaks her word. Now that most of the day has gone by, Aaliyah knows that Lilly will arrive soon. Making sure that her window is still cracked open, she jumps into bed with Graham Cracker at the foot.

Aaliyah says, *"Oh boy, I hope Grandma doesn't notice Abby is missing from the treehouse. She may wonder how my favourite toy disappeared."* She chuckles. *"I may have to say you ate it."* She looks at Graham Cracker.

Graham Cracker says, *"I will definitely get a stern talking to, but if it helps you by not having to explain what happened, then so be it."* Graham Cracker has an "I got your back" kinda look.

Aaliyah says, *"Thanks, buddy. Goodnight."*

Graham Cracker says, *"Goodnight... zzzzzzzzz."*

Aaliyah says, *"Boy, that dog can knock out fast."* She smiles as she pulls the comforter over her shoulders.

Puff... Poof... Lilly twinkles through. She goes over to Aaliyah's bed and whispers, *"Aaliyah, Aaliyah... I'm here..."* Aaliyah opens her eyes, not startled or tickled this time. She has gotten used to the whole twinkle thing.

Aaliyah says, *"I'm so glad you're here. I have so many questions."*

CHAPTER TWELVE

Questions... Answers?

P uff ...poof ... Lilly has arrived. Aaliyah is now awake and eager to have her questions answered.

Aaliyah says, *"I'm so glad you're here, Lilly. I have been so anxious to talk to you. I have so many unanswered questions. Everything happened so fast. I still can't believe what I saw. It looked like something out of a sci-fi movie. Godzilla meets King Kong in Tokyo kinda stuff."*

Lilly, laughing, says, *"I know, and I will answer all your questions and deal with all your concerns. Let me start by telling you how things started. Is that okay, Aaliyah? Then I'll answer any remaining questions you have."*

Aaliyah says, *"Sounds great."*

Lilly begins... *"Long ago, there was an encounter with a sorcerer named Green Eyes. He was eviler than anything you could imagine. He was a lonely, envious, and very bitter sorcerer. He had never found love. He had been rejected by many — not because of his physical appearance, but his heart just wasn't kind. Over the years, his heart hardened and grew angrier and more envious with each day's passing. One day, in a fit of anger, he conjured a fierce spell that would follow his bloodline into the future. This spell had proven to be one of the most powerful of spells. Its powers seemed to grow with time and were even more powerful if someone within his bloodline found true love. You see, the spell was made of jealousy, envy. It's okay to wish for something someone else has; that's only natural. Like you have a dog to play with, and I wish I did. That being said, I wouldn't wish you harm, but Green Eyes was evil and his intention was not good. So Green Eyes, being jealous that he could not find love, cast a spell. He made it so that any descendant of his bloodline would grow hardened and evil with every act of kindness and love. True love, well, if you had found that, the spell would be that much more powerful, as we saw with Dark Madness. If he could not be happy, he wanted no one to be, but he could only conjure up a spell affecting members of his own bloodline. Green Eyes, filled with rage, cast his spell. His isolation and bitterness conjured the spell of spells. Mystical Forest until that time had been always peaceful, calm, beautiful... always. Dark Madness, if it hadn't been for that spell, would have remained a peaceful, loving guy. He was in love with a girl. This is where our two worlds blended. As you know, we have the ability, some of us anyways, to morph into human form. Well, Daryl had morphed and was falling madly in love with a human. Yes, a human."*

Aaliyah says, *"Wow."* She and Graham Cracker are so into the story Lilly is telling them that they remain almost speechless and motionless. They are focused on her words. They are focused on this crazy story.

Lilly continues... *"You see, Dark Madness lived most of his life human. Daryl was his human name, and being so in love with a human, he remained on Planet Earth. He was happy and so in love. He had created a family, and he neither needed nor wanted anything else in life. He was truly happy."*

Graham Cracker says, *"Oh, keep going, please... I need to know more."*

"The woman he had fallen in love with is your aunt. Through that love they shared, they created a child and life was so good for them."

Aaliyah says, *"That's AIZEN, but he looks different. And why haven't I seen my aunt?"*

"I'm getting to that." Lilly goes on to say... *"As the curse continued to take over Daryl's personality, making him one of the most powerful sorcerers since Green Eyes, your Aunt Emily stopped coming to Mystical Forest. It was too painful for her."* Lilly, feeling emotional, looks at Aaliyah with her head tilted and her hands gently under her chin. She looks like she is envisioning something so sweet. Guess she really is. She is thinking about Daryl, Emily, and their once beautiful family.

Snapping out of her memory, she continues, *"He left his family. Over time, the curse took hold, and like his father before him, he became angry and bitter. Pure evil now ran through his veins. The strength or the evil sorcerer and his evil counterparts continued to grow and so did ambitions of putting our lights out. Literally putting them out."*

Aaliyah says, *"So that's why Aizen was weeping. It is his dad that we were battling against."*

"WOWSIE," says Graham Cracker from the corner of the room.

"Yes." Lilly continues, *"Aizen can morph. He has the mystical capabilities from his father. He is the Aizen you know when he is on Planet Earth, just living like a normal little boy. For your aunt's sake we cast a spell, helping her erase the hurtful memories of her Daryl. Well, at least soften the pain. She was aware of what happened to him; she lived it. But when things really started to change, she knew the curse had taken hold. He was no longer her Daryl. We cast a spell to send him far away."*

TAP… TAP… TAP… on the window.

Aaliyah says, *"Who could that be?"* Lilly is also startled.

Aaliyah, moving towards the window, says, *"It's my aunt!"* Aunt Emily twinkles through. Aaliyah asks, *"How is she twinkling?"*

Emily chuckles. *"You see, Aaliyah, Daryl tried to give me powers before the curse took hold. He wanted me to have the powers to survive. He figured that if I had two worlds to choose from, I would pick the safest. I knew that it would probably be my Daryl who would be returning to put our lights out. The thing is, when Daryl cast the spell, it didn't work because I am already from the bloodline of Mystical Forest. Somehow, someone before me was from the Forest but morphed into human and made a life here, and because of that, our bloodline has ties to Mystical Forest. When the evil took my Daryl over and he was now Dark Madness, he was no longer mine. I had to let him go, let it all go, so I could survive. Aizen and I had each other. That gave me purpose. I had to be strong for him."* Emily pauses for a moment, and then she explains, *"I believe the bloodline began with Thérèse."*

Aaliyah remembers, *"Oh, the French grandma with the funny symbols in her name."*

Emily smiles and responds, *"Yes."*

Aaliyah asks, *"Will this happen..."* Now feeling shy, she doesn't want to finish, but she knows she needs to know. *"Will Aizen become evil too?"*

Lilly says, *"We are working on a spell to end the curse forever."* She lowers her head and a tear rolls down her cheek. *"There has been nothing yet, but now we think we are on to something. We hope we will conjure up the spell that can end the curse forever. Maybe even bring back Daryl. After all, he did back down to Aizen."*

Emily says, *"See, sweetheart, it had to be someone from our bloodline, but it couldn't be me because of my relationship with Daryl. That cancelled me out. The fact that Dark Madness shrunk down and disappeared at Aizen's standoff, well, we're very hopeful."*

Aaliyah says, *"That kid, he's gonna get it."* She shakes her head.

Emily asks, *"Who?"*

Aaliyah says, *"Aizen, for being so mean to me. He obviously knew I was Aaliyah, his cousin."*

Emily, laughing, says, *"Yes, I'm sure he did. I guess he figured being younger that he would capitalize on the occasion and get his jabs in. Sorry, Aaliyah."*

Emily continues to answer Aaliyah's questions. Lilly pops in and out of the conversation as well. They talk for some time. Emily goes on to say, *"Remember, humans won't understand all of this. They may even think you have lost all your marbles, that you are loose in the head, that you done lost your mind. Also, we do not know who in our bloodline has awakened their powers. And maybe not all of us have them. There is still so much unknown. Remember, if you start talking about talking dogs and flying unicorns, kids are gonna think you have more than just a great imagination. Never mind telling them you are the Mystical Forest Fairy Princess."* She smiles sweetly. *We will need you again in the future. Dark Madness will return, but will he return as Daryl or Dark* illy chimes in, *"Aaliyah, we have several other dark wizards and sorcerers amongst us. We will need your help again."*

- *THE END* -

"Now that I'm done telling you this story, I can get some rest." Grandma, who is watching from the crack of the door to Aaliyah's bedroom, with a deep yawn, heads to her bedroom. *"GOODNIGHT, MY PRINCESS. GRANDMA KNOWS EVERYTHING."*

Till next time...

CHARACTER LIST

Aaliyah: The Mystical Fairy Princess

Graham Cracker: Aaliyah's trusted canine companion

Grandma: Monique

Sarah: Aaliyah's mom

Dad: Aaliyah's dad

Armani: Aaliyah's brother

Lillyana, also known as Lilly: Fairy who helps guide Aaliyah

Daryl: Dark Madness

Emily: Aaliyah's aunt, Aizen's mom, and Daryl's wife

Aizen: Aaliyah's cousin fairy who is the communicator of Mystical Forest

Grandfather Bob: Grandma Monique's dad

Grandmother Doris: Grandma Monique's mom

Thérèse: Aizen and Aaliyah's Great-Great-Grandma and Monique's grandmother

Abigail, also referred to as Abby: Aaliyah's favourite unicorn stuffie

Rosko: Military Leader of Footmen

Joshua: Head of Criminal Activities

Jill: Head of Communication and Languages

Morgan-Rizzo Transport School workers:

Michelle

John

Samantha and **Peaches the Dragon**

Amanda and **Midnight the Mystical Cat**

Vanessa and **Kora the White Tiger**

CPSIA information can be obtained
at www.ICGtesting.com
Printed in the USA
BVHW062349040921
615878BV00001B/1

9 780228 853091